Make-up Designory's

Character Make-up

by Paul Thompson

First Printing 2005

ISBN 0-9749500-0-9

LCCN 2004091103

Attention Corporations, Universities, Colleges, and Professional Organizations:
Quantity discounts are available on bulk purchases
of this book for educational or gift purposes.
For information, please contact:
Make-up Designory®
129 S. San Fernando Boulevard
Burbank, CA 91502
818-729-9420

Acknowledgments

First and foremost, I wish to thank the students, whose thirst for knowledge has led us to develop and create the curriculum and techniques that are designed to reach the artist in all of them. Without them, we would not have had the dedication to complete this book.

To my colleagues Myles O'Reilly, Karl Zundel, Stephanie Caillabet, and Juliet Loveland whose contributions were numerous, this book would not have been possible without them. Myles' amazing illustrations are only overshadowed by his friendship and willingness to critique and help a fellow artist find his way. Karl's ability to bring clarity to any subject and his vigilant attention to detail has made so many of the processes easy to understand. To the queen of everything hair, Stephanie has been my savior. She is the definition of the word professional. To Juliet who not only helped with the technical edit of this book, but also worked tirelessly to ensure that I was as thorough as possible.

To Peter Lambertz the one man more involved in this book than I am. He is responsible for all things right with this book. I accept responsibility for all the errors. His depth of knowledge has been an asset, both in the creation of the design for the cover and in the supervision of the book's layout. He has meticulously ensured that the overall presentation of this book is logical and maintains continuity. I have to thank the photographers whose photographs made each process clear and who made sure they captured each artist's best work. Derek Althen and Tara Holland's sharp eye made the whole process of shooting each technique easier and a lot more rewarding. I am indebted to Patricia Holland who has spent many hours of her life making sure that what I wrote was actually in English. Additionally, to all the models that allowed each of us to poke, prod, and abuse their faces in the name of education. Their contribution is evident throughout this book. Essential support came from my close friends Tate Holland and John Bailey, who supported this effort every step of the way, sustaining myself and a book written on weekends, nights, holidays, and every other spare moment I could find. To my instructor at Orange Coast College, David Scaglione, who helped me find the make-up artist within myself. Without his teachings and support I would probably not have had the courage to begin a career as a make-up artist.

No one has suffered as much as my family during the writing of this book. They endured all of my frustrations and long nights, without receiving any of the creative rewards. It was a labor of love that would not have been possible without the support of my wife Denyse and my girls, Samantha and Emma.

TABLE OF CONTENTS

TABLE OF CONTENTS

PREFACE

INTRODUCTION TO
CHARACTER MAKE-UP

Every make-up you do is a character make-up, whether it is a horrible monster or an actor portraying a housewife. With the understanding that every make-up should be treated as a character, allow us to explain what is covered in this book.

This book is a step-by-step guide to doing different types of character make-ups. With the emphasis on what we would call special make-up effects rather than on beauty techniques. Character make-up is one of most diversified courses we offer at Make-up Designory. We cover a great many techniques in a very short period of time and are designed to follow a particular path that allows your skills to build upon each other. We are not only trying to teach you how to be a make-up artist, but also how to think like one. Instead of trying to demonstrate everything you might encounter, rather we teach you how to deal with any situation you might face. Of course, the latter is the most ideal way to approach this industry and its infinite possibilities.

This book was written with the principal that each chapter builds on the previous chapter. We start out with the basics of being an artist and how to think properly and finish up with how these types of make-ups are completed. This book focuses on the application of make-up to an actor. We will touch on formulation but as an overview, rather than as a how-to. We suggest practicing each technique immediately following each chapter, as well as practicing each technique multiple times. The book uses photographs to highlight each process, which makes it very easy to follow along. And allows the book to be used as a reference when attempting each technique.

Make-up artistry is a very demanding subject, and requires a total dedication to both practicing the techniques and the quest for more knowledge. The industry is ever changing and you must stay informed and be accepting of the changes that inevitably are going to happen. You'll find that your ability to learn increases ten times when you are enjoying what you are doing.

Chapter 1

Make-up Principles

The Artist

Art is a very diversified subject and encompasses numerous preconceived notions of what an artist is. Many people feel that art is an inherent talent, and that artists are born with some magical gift which allows them to do what they do, when in reality art is a learned skill that is developed into well executed skills. Although some geniuses do exist, such as Leonardo da Vinci and Michel Angelo however most artists are very well practiced normal people. We all start out in life seeing and working as artists, but somewhere in adolescence we stop drawing or painting and start believing that we are not artistic. The people that continue to work through their childhood are the artists most people feel have that magical talent, when in reality they are just well practiced. These skills can be learned at any point in your life, regardless of age. With enough perseverance and lots of practice you can achieve your goals, whether they are to be an artist or a make-up artist.

Highlight and Shadow

Chiaroscuro; which means, the treatment of light and shade in drawing and painting, or what we will call highlight and shadow for the remainder of this book. Classically speaking, the only way to achieve a three dimensional appearance is with highlight and shadow. This is also true of make-up. In fact, every make-up we will do is nothing more than a brilliant execution of highlight and shadow. Even beauty make-up completely revolves around highlight and shadow. In drawing, an artist uses highlight and shadow to create the illusion of the third dimension by manipulating light and shade. The same applies for make-up; well placed shadows can depress an area of the face and conversely a well placed highlight can pull an area of the face forward. Understanding these basic principles of light and shade and how they affect different objects and surfaces is the key to a successful drawing or make-up application. If you look at two objects, the first is a cylindrical block and the second a rectangular block of the same size and width. The outline of the two blocks will give you a clue as to their shape, but it is the way the light reflects off those objects that tells us their true shape. Let us take those same two blocks and cover the ends of each block; this will remove the obvious area

of the block where the shape is easy to define. Next, place a light to the right of each block. Looking at each block we again can tell their individual shape. The rectangular block will have a strong highlight on one side of the block and a strong shadow on the other side of it, creating a sharp division between the two surfaces, whereas, the cylindrical block will slowly transition from a strong highlight to a strong shadow. The two blocks are being hit by the light and that light is then reflected into your eye. Because the cylindrical block is round the light is reflecting off the surface differently as that surface slowly turns away from the light. This indicates the surface is curved. On the rectangular block the right side of the block is angled towards the light source, so that entire side is receiving and reflecting equal amounts of light. The back side of the block is completely turned away from the light source, thus that side is completely dark. This indicates that the object has a corner. The two examples apply to every aspect of drawing, painting, and make-up. Whenever you are trying to create the illusion of depth you will apply one or both of these principles.

Before we are able to understand that highlight and shadow are everything to an artist we must first begin to think and see as an artist. To do this we must do what some call "slipping into a right brain type of thought". A great book about this subject is "Drawing on the Right side of the Brain" by Betty Edwards. They do not mean drawing on the correct side of the brain, but rather they have tried to identify a region of the brain that controls our creativity and artistic abilities; whereas the left side of the brain is for communication, mathematics, and anything else analytical. The basic concept of the book is not how to draw but how to see. You will learn that this drawing, painting and sculpting thing is a learned skill rather than an inherent talent. People that do have talent are not necessarily born with it, but are actually just well-practiced. Art is a learned skill that can be successfully executed by just about anyone. Look at your nose in a mirror, then look at one eye, perceiving neither one as an actual eye or nose, but visualizing them as the shapes that make up the eye and the nose. Throw out those useless terms that we use to communicate and replace them with seeing that allows us to look at a thing (that thing formally known as a nose) and understand that it is curved here and straight there; it has roundness and looks a bit cylindrical.

We use aging to help us teach these basic concepts, and will be focusing on aging each other rather than making everyone old. There are three techniques for aging an actor. The first is a two-dimensional technique with just color or, as we like to call it, highlight and shadow. This two dimensional technique is also known as Paint and Powder make-up. Paint and Powder make-up is the process of creating the illusion of age with make-up alone. The second is utilizing latex to create actual three dimensional wrinkles in the skin as opposed to just creating the illusion with color. This technique is called Aging Stipple, which refers to the way the latex is applied. And the third and final technique is to use prosthetic appliances to create any age you like. Prosthetics are the most versatile of the three and can be used on just about anyone to create almost any age.

Sculptural Light

This is the perfect time to introduce the concepts of sculptural light. An artist that paints portraits has the ability to select the light source for his painting and the skill to position it anywhere he wants. Now this doesn't mean he paints a lamp in the picture, it means he highlights and shadows the face according to the position of the light. If he doesn't highlight and shadow his drawing according to his light source, his painting will not look very real. As make-up artists, we are faced with a similar situation, however we do not have the ability to place that light anywhere we want. We must always place it in front and above our model. The main reason is the performer is moving and acting within a three dimensional world. If we did move the light source, we would have funny shadows all over the face. So when asked where to place a highlight or a shadow, the answer lies within another question: where is the light? Once you understand where the light source is (always in front and above the actor) you should always know where to paint your highlight and shadows. This concept is probably the most understated concept in make-up, yet it is absolutely essential to proper placement of your highlights and shadows. It is the difference between an okay make-up and a great make-up.

The Two Dimensional World

It is of the utmost importance that you fully understand the difference between the three-dimensional world and the two-dimensional world of film and TV. Again, turn towards a mirror and you will see that the image of yourself is really flat and shapeless. Also notice that you can only see exactly half of yourself. You are seeing yourself two-dimensionally. Next, hold your finger in front of your face and close one eye, then open that eye and close the other eye. Your finger will move from side to side as you switch eyes. This is happening because we have two eyes enabling us to tell depth and see, sort of, around objects. In essence, we have the ability to see more than half the object. Height, width, and depth are the three dimensions that we see in. A three-dimensional camera is actually two cameras bolted together at the same distance apart as human eyes. The right side records in one color and the left side records in another color, so when an object is placed in front of the cameras, the right camera is shooting it from the same perspective as our right eye would, then, when we go to the movies we have to wear those funny glasses, and it is these glasses that allow only the info that we want to reach the proper eye. In other words, the right eye only sees what the right camera recorded. The illusion is then completed in our mind. A regular camera records everything through one lens and is projected onto a flat wall or shown on a flat screen. That is why Film and TV are only two-dimensional. We do not have the ability to tell depth. What this means for a make-up artist is that we can fool the audience into believing they are seeing something that may only be painted on the face as opposed to really being there. They do not have the ability to really see the depth but rather the illusion of depth created by us.

Color

As artists we must have a firm understanding of color, sometimes viewed as a magical element that only gifted artists are able to grasp. There has been a great deal written about color and we are going to try to explain it as simply as possible. There are three aspects of color, Hue, Intensity, and Value. Hue is the name of the color. Value pertains to how light or dark a color looks. And Value is the amount of gray a color has in it.

The next thing to understand is the color wheel. There are three primary colors, red, blue and yellow. There are three secondary colors: red mixed with blue equals purple, blue mixed with yellow equals green, and yellow mixed with red equals orange; if you arrange these colors in a circle with the respective primaries between the proper secondaries you have the color wheel. Further, if you mix the secondary colors with the primaries you get another color between each secondary and primary. Mixing red and purple gives you a red purple. Mixing purple with blue gives you violet. Mixing blue with green gives you a blue green. Mixing green with yellow gives you a yellow green. Mixing yellow with orange gives you a yellow orange. Mixing orange with red gives you a red orange. You now have a completed color wheel. If you pick a color on the color wheel and then look directly across from that color you will find that particular color's complimentary color. White and black can now be added to every color to create tints of that color. White, of course, will make the color lighter and duller, but the resulting color will not be as vibrant as the original color prior to adding white. Black does the opposite of white and makes colors darker. Again when using black to alter a color you wind up with a less vibrant color.

In cosmetics we can apply these same rules to color. However, when using cosmetics you are less likely to be applying a true primary or secondary. Normally, we are using some form of those colors so this color theory should be kept in mind when combining make-ups. Note that black is usually a really dark blue or green, when talking about cosmetics, so be careful how you use it.

Sanitation

As a make-up artist, sanitation is a very important part of maintaining a clean and professional environment. The cleanliness of you and your station is the first step in conveying competence to an actor.

First, let's talk about you. Always maintain a clean and neat appearance. Hand sanitizer should be at your station at all times and should be utilized in between each actor. After eating or smoking, you should wash your hands with soap and water, as well as consider brushing your teeth.

Next, your tools. All brushes should be cleaned with brush cleaner immediately after each use. Do not wait till you have another actor to work on.   Sponges and powder puffs should only be used on one performer and thrown away after each use. You may choose to maintain a sponge or a puff inside a Zip-lock bag for a single performer. This is acceptable as long as they are thrown away at the end of the day. Disposable mascara wands are just that, disposable, and should never be returned to a mascara container after touching any part of the face.

Combs and hairbrushes need to be chemically sanitized with

Barbicide or bleach solution. Also known as quats, Barbicide comes in a concentrate and needs to be diluted with water. Mix 1/2 cup Barbicide with 1 gallon of water. The temperature of the water is not a factor. For the bleach solution, mix 1/4 cup bleach with 1 gallon of water. Again, the temperature is not a factor. Both solutions are good for a period of 24 hours only and must be thrown out after that time.

Combs and hairbrushes are to be sanitized after each use. They are never to be used on more than one person without being sanitized. Remove hair from the comb or brush, rinse with water, and drop into either of the solutions. Leave immersed for no less than ten minutes, then remove and rinse with clean water, and allow to dry.

Make-up should be scooped from its container with a palette knife and placed onto a palette. Work from the palette, not from the container. The palette can be cleaned with 99% alcohol before working on your next performer. For pressed powders, where it is impossible to scoop out product, you will have to spritz the make-up with 99% alcohol to sanitize it. The nice thing about powder products is the low chance of bacteria growing in the container. A good rule of thumb, is to remove the product from the container before applying it.

Pencils are sharpened to clean them. The sharpener can be cleaned with 99% alcohol. If anything falls onto the floor, it is no longer sanitized and needs to be cleaned. This also goes for sneezing or coughing on an item.

Morgues

A morgue is not only a place to keep dead people, it is also, for the make-up artist, a vast reference book of pictures and photographs. You cannot purchase this book, you have to build it. It doesn't really matter what area of make-up you are learning or interested in, the idea is to create a book of reference that pertains to what you may need to do in the future.

Creating sections in the book will help you organize the pictures into easy-to-find sections. Categories could include, but are not limited to, men, women, children, old people, bald people, facial hair, hair styles, monsters, animals, mythical characters, prosthetics, historical characters, wardrobe, critters, creatures, sculptures, statues, and injuries.

This morgue should be a separate book or binder from any notes, and it is completely up to you how well organized you make it. The use of acetate sheet protectors will keep your pictures nice or they can be glued to a piece of construction paper.

Finding the pictures you will need for your morgue is a little harder. It will become an ongoing process for you, eventually filling a bookshelf as opposed to just one binder. Magazines, as well as newspapers are a great picture source, however you may need to buy specialty magazines to find specific photos. Or you can just go through all your magazines and pull out the photos you need for the specific sections. Try to find as many real pictures as possible. It is our job to recreate reality and the only way to do that is to reference reality.

Tools of the Trade

The following is the essential list of tools with a description of what each tool is required for and how it is used. These items are the tools you will be using to create just about every type of character make-up.

Brush Roll- Fabric brush holder that holds several brushes. It has a soft cover to help protect the bristle ends of the brushes and rolls into a tight roll for easy storage.

Brushes- A tool with hair or fibers imbedded into it, utilized by artist for painting.

White Sponges- A soft foam latex sponge used to apply cream make-up.

Orange Sponge- A porous sponge used to apply cream make-up in a textured fashion.

Black Sponge- A heavily porous sponge used to apply cream make-up in a textured fashion. This sponge comes in three styles: fine, medium and coarse.

Palette Knife- A metal artist spatula used to scoop make-up out of a make-up container and to sculpt wax or blend edge.

Tissue- A disposable piece of thin, soft, and absorbent paper.

Powder Puffs- A velour puff used to powder make-up.

Tweezers- Used to tweeze hairs and hold fluttery edges.

Mirror- A hand held mirror should be made available for the actors so they may see what you are doing throughout the process of making them up, especially if there is no large mirror at your disposal.

Utility Scissors- A large sharp pair of scissors used for everything from cutting sponges to cutting into a bottle. These scissors should be very strong and durable.

Good Scissors- A small or more precise type of scissors used for cutting hair or a bald cap. These should not be used as a general cutting tool and should not be used on sponges. Sponges dull scissors faster than anything else that a make-up artist may be cutting.

Comb- A standard barber comb can be used for a wide variety of situations from prepping hair for a bald cap to combing a fake beard. You may choose to purchase a set of combs to allow yourself a little variety and versatility.

Brush- Mainly used on people with lots of hair. Again a couple of sizes and styles will provide you with flexibility.

Cotton Swabs- A stick with a small cotton ball on the end. Any type or style will do, however, we recommend the six inch wooden handle swab. finding it more versatile than the average small swab.

Cotton Balls- Perfect for removing make-up or adhesive, are one of the softest products you can use on a performer's face.

Make-up Pads- These are cotton pads used to remove make-up, and are used in a similar way to a cotton ball with the exception they are a little more durable.

Make-up Box- A make-up kit. Can be made of wood, plastic, or aluminum. Each one has different features and it is completely a matter of personal choice and preference as to which one is best.

Set Bag- A medium sized bag usually having many side compartments for bottles and tools. It can also be a small individual bag used for the tools and touch up materials needed for only one performer.

Bald Cap Form- A plastic form used to create a bald cap. May be smooth or textured.

Container for Brush Cleaner- A small bottle with a lid used to clean your brushes. This bottle is designed to be used at your station with the contents being discarded at the end of each day.

Brush Holder- A plastic, metal, or glass cup used to hold your brushes upright. This is the preferred method of holding brushes. You don't want to use your brush roll because it is easily soiled.

Cotton Swab Holder- Same as a brush holder.

Hackle- A square piece of wood with metal spikes sticking out of it. It is used to detangle loose hair.

Utility Tweezers- A less expensive pair that can be used to tear latex on a burn.

Mints- Everyone needs fresh breath. Gum may annoy some performers.

Hand Sanitizer- Any professional sanitizer or Sea Breeze to clean your hands.

Placemats- A disposable mat used to ensure a sanitary work space.

Cover Cloth- A clean cover to protect the actor's wardrobe from accidental spills.

Make-up Pencil Sharpener- A metal sharpener, of course, used to sharpen your pencils. It is also used to sanitize your pencils.

Spray Bottle- Mainly for water, but can be used for just about any liquid. Use it to wet hair or make an actor look sweaty.

Hair Clips- Metal clips used to hold hair back out of the way.

Hair Bands- Coated rubber bands to tie back hair

Airbrush- A tool used to spray make-up onto a performer.

Compressor- A mechanical device used to supply air to the airbrush. A small silent type is best.

Pipe Cleaners- Used to clean the small openings and parts of the airbrush.

Tooth Brush- Used to scrub those difficult paints off the airbrush, and can be used to flick texture onto a make-up.

Thinning Shears- Special scissors used to thin hair.

Curling Irons- Hot irons used to style hair. A variety of sizes are needed depending on the type of beard you are laying.

Metal Comb- Same as a standard barber comb except it is made of metal and will not melt if touched by the curling iron.

Disposable Mascara Wands- A sanitary wand for applying mascara.

Eyebrow Brush- A small brush, a tooth brush will also work, to style the eyebrow and to clean make-up out of it.

1 oz. Plastic Cups- A thick plastic cup used for all liquids. In order to keep everything sanitary as you use it, this cup enables you to limit the amount of liquid you pour at a time, allowing for double dipping.

Wide Mouth Plastic Cups- Larger cups than the one ounce allowing for larger objects like a sponge to be dipped into the cup.

Finger Nail Clippers- For cutting nails. Nice to have for a performer if they are needed. A small kit is perfect for you to maintain your hygiene.

10 cc Syringe- A syringe without a needle used to dispense blood accurately.

Orange Wood Stick- A wooden stick that is beveled at both ends to form a wedge. It is normally used on cuticles, but can be adapted to just about any use.

Styptic Pencil- A small pencil looking object that will help stop the bleeding of small razor cuts.

Razor- An electric or disposable razor for those performers who need to shave. If you use the disposable type you will also need shaving cream; it is usually best to have both types.

Contact Lens Kit and Eye Drops- A compact set that a performer can use to clean their contact lenses.

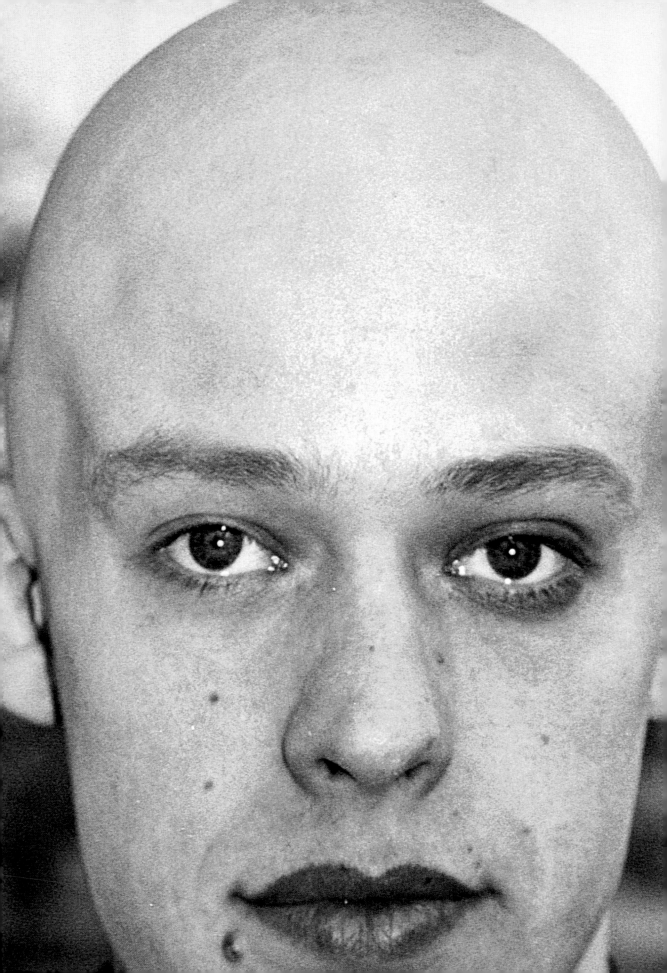

Chapter 2

Anatomy

Understanding the face and how it is structured is an important aspect of being a make-up artist. It is not important to commit all of this information to memory, but rather look at this as an overview that can be referenced whenever necessary.

The Bones

The following is a frontal and side view of the skull. It shows the placement of all the general highlight and shadows. It also illustrates the skull configuration and the terms associated with it. The location and the way the bones of the face are shaded and highlighted are a direct result of their shape and position. Looking at the front view of the human skull you can see how the different bones are shaded with our light source coming from above.

The side view shows how the light reflects off the bones when the light source is from above. In make-up we have to assume the light source is from above, because our actors are moving around in a three dimensional world.

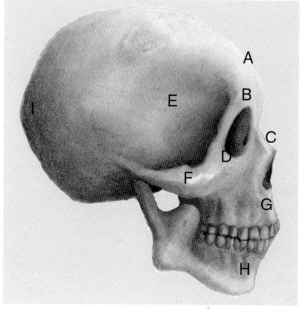

A. Frontal Bone   **B.** Superciliary Ridge
C. Nasal Bone   **D.** Malar Bone
E. Temporal Fossa   **F.** Zygomatic Arch
G. Superior Maxillary Bone   **H.** Inferior Maxillary Bone
I. Occipital

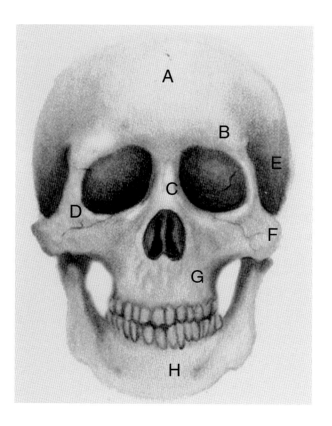

A. Frontal Bone   **B.** Superciliary Ridge
C. Nasal Bone   **D.** Malar Bone
E. Temporal Fossa   **F.** Zygomatic Arch
G. Superior Maxillary Bone   **H.** Inferior Maxillary Bone

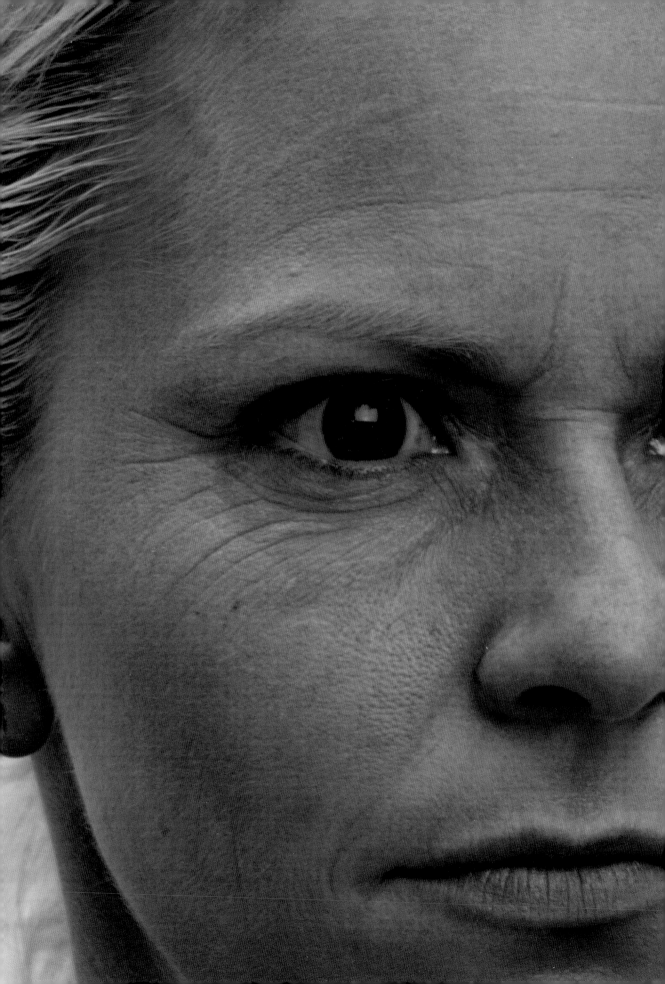

Chapter 3

Aging

The purpose of this section, and the entire book, is to educate you in the theories of highlight and shadow. In this section we will be dealing more with concepts that pertain to aging, and why we do aging techniques, for films and television.

The Process

An aging make-up has many steps and the following is the process of creating age through the use of color. It is not simply the application of make-up to draw on wrinkles and age spots, but an entire process that requires a great deal of finesse.

The first step to this make-up, and to any make-up you do from now until you retire, is analyzing the face. As artists we must first identify what areas we can use and exploit. If the make-up is intended for the theater then you will use what the performer has to offer, creating whatever else you may need in order to get the appropriate age across to the audience. If this make-up is intended for film and TV then we have to be very careful not to do too much. This type of make-up is really best when making the performer only 10 to 15 years older, as trying to make the performer older than that will only cause the make-up to look stagey and unrealistic.

We start with the general highlights and shadows, which are those large highlight and shadows that show off muscle and bone structure.

General Highlight & Shadow of the Forehead & Temples

The emphasis is on the general highlights and shadows of the forehead and not on the wrinkles, so the way to approach this area is to think about how foreheads are formed. What shapes are contained within? How are male and female skulls different? First, the male skull is usually larger and has a more prominent brow structure than a female skull; thus the male skull usually has more dips and depressions than a female skull. Start with a shadow, Shadow #4 in the Mud Palette, placing it in the temple area. The temple area is a depression found just above the cheekbone, just behind the eye socket, and just below the frontal bone. This fossa or depression is turned away from our imaginary light source so it can be fairly dark. If you look at our gray scale sheets this shadow should start out at 8 and blend out to a 5. It should

be applied as a soft shadow. Blending on both sides, however, it should remain darkest closest to the bones. If you are having a hard time understanding what these bones look like and where they are placed, you can refer to Chapter 2. A soft highlight, Hilight in the Mud Palette, should be placed on all the high surfaces such as the cheekbone, the eye socket, and the edge of the frontal bone. The lightest spot of the highlight should be closest to the imaginary light source. There is another area of the forehead that must be shadowed, however most students overdo this shadow. (It lies between the brow bone and the round area that makes up the center of the forehead.) Now in reality the shadow is being cast by that round area and should be shaded as if you are trying to create a sphere in the middle of the forehead. Since this shadow is so close to our imaginary light source, which we covered so well in our sculptural light section, the shadow should start at about #4 and blend out to #2 on our gray scale. Then of course, highlight the very top of the sphere in the middle of the forehead as well as the brow bone. Again, all of the general highlights and shadows of the forehead should be soft.

General Highlight & Shadow of the Eyes

This area of the face could easily go too dark, making the performer look sick. Use Shadow #4 and Hilight from the mud palette. Visualize the eye area, to perceive it the way we want it to appear. Allow your mind to see the depressions in the face. Take the shadow and apply it along the crease of the eye, but be careful not to overdo it. In some situations, you should allow that crease area to remain untouched, such as if the model's eyes are already dark and adding any more darkness would take the effect too far. Next, shadow above the lid and emphasize the fatty tissue area. On each person it's going to be a little different, so shade just enough to create roundness to the bottom of the fatty tissue area. Do not correct the eye area. Next, shade under the eye bag giving it the very beginnings of more fullness. A great technique is to not draw a line of shadow completely under the eye bag but rather do a small bit of shading in each corner of the bag and allow the illusion to be created in the minds of the viewers. Again we are not creating wrinkles, so the emphasis is on the general shapes. Using Hilight, and remembering exactly where our imaginary light source is, we should then apply highlights to the fatty tissue area up close to the eyebrow. The lightest spot of highlight should be the spot closest to the light source. Now, highlight the bag in the same fashion. (The crease needs to be highlighted a little differently.) Directly below the crease you will notice a raised area – this area should be soft highlight that begins to form the top of the nasolabial fold.

General Highlight & Shadow of the Cheekbone

The performer's face structure is what dictates how we do the cheeks. The first one is the gaunt look, which we follow with shading the structure of the cheekbone up under the eye socket and down into the hollow of the cheek. The second is on a person with a fuller face in which the cheekbone is not well defined. With this type, with shadow simply push the area right in front of the ear in. The third type is a strong cheekbone on a person who is not really thin. In this case, the shading will follow under the cheekbone and up under the apple of the cheek. In each instance you will highlight the cheekbone and the other high areas, but remember that you are endeavoring to create roundness, not trying to achieve an uplifting beauty cheek. Apply the shading in each example as hash marks rather than as a smooth nice application. You want this shadow to be broken up and uneven.

With each of these areas we are building onto the next area. So as you do the cheek see how it relates to the temple and to the eye area.

General Highlight & Shadow of the Jaw-line

There are actually only a couple of types. And what we are really trying to create is a jowl or two. A common mistake you must be careful to avoid is not connecting the corner of the mouth to the jowl. Really, mostly highlight and very small amounts of shading create a sphere like shape along the jaw line, which makes up the jowl. The shadow is applied in a small triangle shape on the edge of jaw line separating the chin from the rest of the jaw. Do not just create this on every person you work on, but try to use whatever their particular face may offer in terms of some sort of beginning to this jowl. And again tie the jowl into the cheek.

General Highlight & Shadow of the Neck

As with the cheekbone the weight and facial structure of the performer is going to dictate what style will be used. In most cases just follow what the performer has. For example, if the performer's neck is very thin it will show off every muscle in the neck, providing us with a lot of areas to highlight and shadow. If the performer's neck is really full then maybe all we will be able to do is highlight. Remember we will do more with the neck when we do wrinkles.

Wrinkle Techniques

Since the nasolabial fold is usually the largest wrinkle on the face, it is the best place to illustrate how a wrinkle should be done. Every wrinkle is made up of two highlights and one shadow. The rules of sculptural light still apply to a wrinkle as it would apply to the general highlights and shadows. First, place the shadow, Shadow #4 in the Mud Palette, into the crease of the fold and blend up and away from the mouth. Emphasize that the shadow is applied exactly the same as if you were trying to create a cylinder. Apply the darkest shadow along the edge of the crease. If we apply the gray scale formula that we did on our highlight and shadow worksheets, 10 would be right at the crease and 9 would be just above that then 8 and so on. This shadow would also be considered a hard edge, because one side has a sharp edge and the other side is blended out. As the shadow moves away from the crease it begins to turn towards our light source and, of course, starts to turn into a highlight. A sharp edge of highlight, Hilight in the Mud Palette, is then placed below the crease and blended towards the mouth. This area is a highlight because it is directly exposed to our light source. The last area to contend with is the area the shadow turns into a highlight, so as the shadow slowly ends, the highlight slowly starts. This highlight is considered a soft highlight, and as the highlight gets closer to the light source it becomes the lightest color. On the gray scale worksheet that color would be #1.

All wrinkles are done in this exact same fashion, with a sharp edge of shadow right at the crease, and blended up, then a sharp edge of highlight is applied right below the shadow at the crease and blended down. Finally a soft highlight is applied above the shadow. This is the anatomy of a wrinkle and when doing stage make-up you can pretty much put them wherever you desire, as long as you follow the facial structure and proper human anatomy. For a film or TV make-up you should only do this effect in existing wrinkles that you wish to deepen.

The whole trick to drawing on wrinkles is not to draw them on. Follow what the performer has to offer and if they are particularly wrinkle free then create the wrinkles with just highlight. The highlight allows you to draw the wrinkles on without it becoming overdone. Remember using this technique of aging, you will only be able to age the person realistically 10 to 15 years older.

Stippling Techniques

The first step is to match the performer's skin color with a base color, then mix a lighter version of that base color and then a darker version. Sounds simple enough but how in the world do we match a performer's skin color? Base matching is an art form that requires a bit of explanation. There are two types of undertone on the planet, one is ruddy or red and the other is a greenish yellow or olive. Now what does that mean? Well, the olive color of skin is the most common found and most likely to be you. Look into a mirror and study the colors you see in your face. You should notice that our faces are made up of many colors as opposed to just one color. What you should look at is that color that lies just beneath the surface, not the surface color. We are referring to that color you see in your neck and the color under that surface red. The color you see will either be greenish-yellow or a light red color. Now 95% of the population of the planet is olive while the other 5% is ruddy. When analyzing the face of the performer, this question must be asked of yourself: Is the performer ruddy or olive? If olive, then all the base colors you should be looking at in terms of a base color should be olive. We would love to give you a simple system of determining which colors to use on an olive person, but unfortunately we can't. Every manufacturer of base color uses different methods of determining which colors are deemed olive. However, you may have to do this base match in rubber mask grease paints, which of course have no neat system. The best thing to do is take all of your base colors out and simply look at the colors. You will very quickly be able to identify which colors are olive and which are ruddy.

Once you have established which undertone the performer is, the next thing is to ask yourself, are they light or dark? So grab the color you think best matches their lightness or darkness and correct undertone and apply it along the jaw line. This will allow you to see how the base color matches the performer's neck. More than likely you will have to alter this color to make it match perfectly.

At this moment I should mention something about color. Let's take the mystery out of color and make it a completely manageable concept, a concept that you will never forget and will always be able to use in every color situation. There are three primary colors and they are red, blue, and yellow. These three colors make up every color you see, including base colors. White is the absence of color and black is an abundance of color. With these five colors we can make anything. For example we can create all the secondary colors by mixing two of every combination of primary colors. Red and yellow make orange, yellow and blue make green, and blue and red make purple. If we mix all the primaries together you will get brown, by adding white to that and you get beige, which is also known as a base color. By altering how much red or how much yellow we add to this mixture we are able to change the base color from ruddy to olive. Further, we can alter the lightness or the darkness by adding white to lighten it, or a dark brown to darken it.

Getting back to our base match you can choose a color that is very close to the persons face color then, by adding white, brown, red, or yellow, you can alter it in any way you like.

Now that we have determined the base match of our performer, mix a small amount of brown into it and create a darker version of our base color. With the darker base color stipple it, with an orange sponge, into all the general shadow areas. Make sure you round off the sponge with a pair of scissors before you start so you don't end up with any bizarre lines in your make-up. Allow a small amount of the darker base to be stippled out beyond the shadow areas and into the highlights. Next take the Lighter Base color, which was created by adding white to our original base color, and stipple it into the highlight area and again allow that light color to be stippled out into the shadows. The base match is then stippled over the entire make-up. This will help to even out the colors slightly. Next apply a small amount of a mustard yellow color over the highlights. It can be mixed with base or just applied carefully. This color should be applied unevenly. Then do the same with a green color. These colors add those necessary colors to make our make-up look like skin and give it the illusion of translucency. Lastly add a red oxide color, not bright red, to give the skin the required redness. Apply to the end of the nose, to the ears, and to any other area you want more warmth. Every one of these colors you add is creating a small dotted pattern over the face, with each one helping to create that realistic look of skin.

You can either powder in the end or you can do it between each color. If the colors are mixing too much then you should powder between each one.

Vein Work

For blue veins I personally use a Teal Professional Pencil and make squiggly lines on the skin. Keep it very light; the idea is that we are seeing these veins under the skin. You can also use a brush acquiring the make-up from the pencil. And of course you can always go back and soften the pencil lines with a brush. For capillaries I use the Lake Red Pencil. If it is hard enough it can be used straight onto the skin, but usually the Lake Red Pencil is soft so use a small brush and take the make-up from the pencil, then apply it to the skin. Use a small amount of 99% alcohol with the brush to get a very thin translucent line. Skin Illustrator has great vein and capillary colors, but be very careful using an alcohol-based product. If you use too much alcohol, it may run all the other make-up colors together.

Age Spots

I use an eyeliner brush that I mush a little (mush, a technical term for smashing the bristles into a fanned out pattern), then stipple Liverspot #1 & #2 (from the Mud Palette) into the forehead area, creating a light spotted texture. Be very careful, a little goes a long way. The dark color is applied first, then the lighter one is stippled around and on top of the dark one. The idea is to create spots that are more texture than actual spots.

Hair-graying Techniques

Hair white is a funny material. Everyone makes it but for the most part it looks just like every other cream make-up on the market, which means you can purchase a separate hair white or you can simply use a cream product you already own. There are several good liquid hair whites and grays that can be used in combination or alone. Don't use straight white on the hair as it will look artificial. Use a light yellow on red hair, a light orange on black hair and an off white on blonde and brown hair. Starting at the base of the hair, brush the color up away from the skin. Do the whole strand of hair, being careful not to get the make-up on the skin. Do the whole piece, all the way to the tip. You can do as much of the hair as you like. Style is completely left up to you and to what type of "do" your character should be sporting.

Step 2

General highlight is next; using a large brush or a textured sponge stipple into the same general areas we applied shadow. Mix a small amount of the performer's base color into the highlight; about five to ten percent should do. Again, this will custom tint the highlight for the performer. Make the areas closest to the light source the strongest, then less as the highlight moves closer to the shadow.

Aging Step-By-Step

We have photographed a complete paint & powder make-up to illustrate how to put all these elements together. To show the process we made up half the face.

The model with no make-up on.

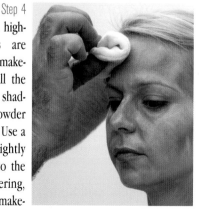

Step 3

The general highlights and shadows are covered very thoroughly earlier in this chapter. As you can see, just with the general highlights and shadows applied, the face is very droopy looking.

Step 1

We begin with the general shadows. Mix a small amount of the performer's base color to the shadow; about five to ten percent will do. This will give you a shadow color that is custom colored for the performer. Do all of the general shadows at one time, starting at the top and working your way down. The forehead shadows are first then the temple. Shadow the eye area then move into the cheek area. Shadow the nose, nasolabial folds, and the jaw line. Lastly, shadow the neck.

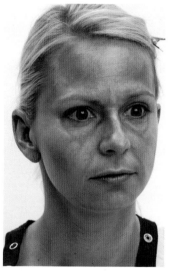

Step 4

Once all the general highlight and shadows are applied, powder the make-up to set it. Once all the general highlight and shadows are applied, powder the make-up to set it. Use a powder puff and lightly press the powder into the make-up. By powdering, you will ensure the make-up you use for the wrinkles does not mix with the general highlights and shadows.

Use the shadow color straight, without any base mixed in. This will give the shadow a darker look than the general shadows. Because we are doing a wrinkle we want it to have a stronger look. For the shadow aspect of the wrinkle, paint on a sharp line of shadow into the existing crease of the forehead. Then blend the color up away from the crease leaving a hard edge of color on the bottom and a soft blending of color on top.

Step 8

The nasolabial fold is also a wrinkle and should be treated in the same way as all the other wrinkles. Note that the nasolabial fold starts behind the nostril and can extend down past the corner of the mouth. However, it should not touch the corner of the mouth.

Step 6

Using the actor's face as a guide to paint in wrinkle lines wherever a slight or light wrinkle is starting to form. Careful of painting the wrinkles on wherever you want, you will find aging the actor looks better when you follow her features.

Step 9

Shadow wrinkles are now added to the model's face. Again, all the shadow part of the wrinkles are done prior to using any highlight. If you are doing a theater production, more shadow lines can be applied if desired.

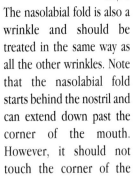

Step 7

The same principle applies to every line, sharp edge on the bottom and a soft edge on top. The lines can be applied around the eyes, in front of the ears, on the neck, and in the corners of the mouth. If the actor is old enough you might even paint them on the lips.

Step 10

Highlight is used without any base color mixed in. This will allow this highlight to stand out a little more prominently. Just like with the shadow, start at the top of the face and work down into the neck. Apply a line of highlight color under the shadow wrinkle, and then blend it down away from the shadow color. The highlight line should extend slightly beyond the end of the shadow line. This will help the wrinkle to thin out at the edges.

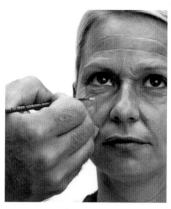

Step 11

Highlight is added to all the wrinkles, accentuating every wrinkle shadow. The highlight is placed first, below the shadow, creating a sharp line between each of them; it is then blended downward. A soft highlight is placed above every wrinkle to create the fullness of the wrinkle.

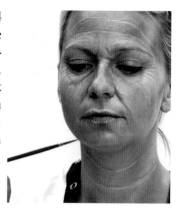

Step 14

Again, highlight lines are very effective to create wrinkle texture to the neck area. Follow the lines in the neck and make sure you do them lightly and close together. The more lines the better in this case.

Step 12

Highlight lines can be used alone to create texture. These lines can only be created with highlight and should be kept thin and light. This technique is ideal to create those fine wrinkle lines found around the more pronounced wrinkles. These same lines also help to achieve a sagging fleshy appearance. You can apply these types of lines around the eyes, in front of the ears, over the lips, and on the neck.

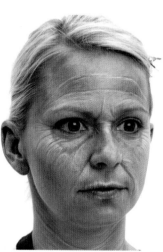

Step 15

The finished highlights and shadows as well as all the wrinkles. The make-up at this point looks really severe and a bit heavy. Now we must add all the flesh tones that are going to make our actor look more human.

Step 13

Highlight lines can be applied to the lips whether or not you applied shadow lines. The lines do a really nice job of defusing the youthful lip line. Depending on how old you are making the actor will depend on how old you make the lips.

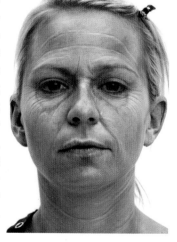

Step 16

Again, powder all the wrinkles first to set them; powder will also ensure the lines will not mix with the base colors. (You may look at this make-up and say that the model looks a lot older than a mere ten to fifteen additional years.) The next step is going to lessen the look of the aging. It may take you a few attempts to achieve a happy medium between how heavy or light to apply the highlights and shadows compared to how heavy you apply the texture

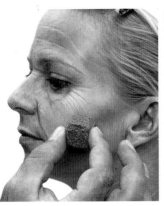

Step 17

Prior to starting this make-up it is important to match the performer's base color to her face. A darker version of that color is stippled into the general shadows, this will soften the shadows and start to blend the overall look.

Step 18

Now mix a lighter version of the performer's base color and stipple it into the highlight areas. Be very careful when applying both these base colors not to eradicate all your wrinkles and fine lines. These colors start to return the model's face to a more natural color.

Step 19

The base match is then stippled, using an orange sponge, over the entire face and neck. When doing a make-up of this nature it is very important to always look at it as a complete character and not just as face make-up. That means you will always make up the neck and ears.

Step 20

The base colors soften the look or the intensity of the highlights and shadows, creating a textured look that simulates real skin. Powder is used to set the base colors. Lightly powder using a colorless powder. Layering the make-up with powder between layers creates a transparent look.

Step 21

Various colors such as green, yellow, and red are mixed with the base match and stippled into areas of the face. Look at real pictures of old people to see where some of these colors are placed. These colors will help create translucency to your make-up even when in reality, it can be thick or opaque.

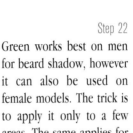

Step 22

Green works best on men for beard shadow, however it can also be used on female models. The trick is to apply it only to a few areas. The same applies for the yellow or mustard color. A brick red color can be used straight or mixed with bases. Apply it to the end of the nose and to the cheeks.

Step 23

A teal professional pencil is used to create veins. Veins are not necessarily an effect of old age but they do help to add realism to your make-up by again adding translucency. Use a really light touch as you do not want a heavy blueness. Apply the veins to the tem-

ple area. The neck is also an area you can add veins. Under the eyes is another location you add uneven sporadic veins.

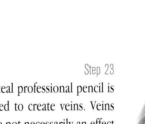

Step 24

Capillaries are used to show aging since the older we get the more likely they are to appear. Capillaries can also be used to show character traits such as a heavy drinker. The capillaries are applied with a brush. Rub the lake red pencil, or any dark red make-up you prefer, onto your palette and then dip your brush into 99% alcohol and lightly apply small and thin squiggly lines to the face. Capillaries can be applied anywhere you want; ears, cheeks, and the nose can receive a higher concentration of them.

Step 25

A small amount of translucent powder is used to set the whole make-up and to complete the look.

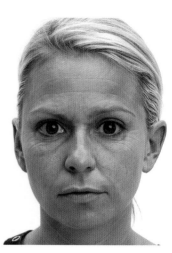

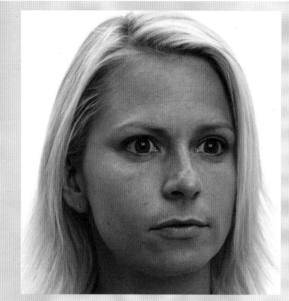

Before

After

The finished side of the face. When doing make-up remember we are aging the performer believably and not painting her old; the after photograph is sagging more than the before photograph and it appears as if gravity is starting to pull down on her skin.

Notes:

Overlay Drawing

Before you ever open your make-up case or touch a brush to an actor's face, you should have a well thought out plan for the make-up. An overlay drawing is the way a make-up artist visualizes a character two dimensionally. This applies even in a situation that only requires you to make an actress more beautiful. Whether you are doing an eye treatment for a beauty make-up or an elaborate old age make-up, an overlay drawing will give you the ability to design and plan out every aspect of a particular make-up.

There are two reasons you would do a drawing of this nature, which is essentially a tracing of the actor's face from a headshot with the changes made to it. The first is to give a producer or a production company a clear-cut idea of what you are planning to do to the actor. The second is to create a design that can be followed by you or other artists.

There are two different ways of creating this for a production. One way is to lay a piece of tracing paper over the picture of the actor, then do the drawing with colored pencils. The other way is to scan the actor's photo into a computer using a program called PhotoShop to create the effects you want.

The following is a step-by-step description of how an overlay drawing is done.

To start you will need an 8"x10" of the actor, some colored pencils, and a pad of tracing paper. Remember, you don't have to worry about which type of make-up or technique you will use to actually age the actor. This is the design phase that will illustrate what the model should look like in her eighties and enable the production company to see how she will look like in their film.

Step 1

Use an 8"x10" photograph of our actor, usually provided by the production company. For the purpose of learning the process, use a photo of yourself, a photo of someone famous, or possibly a friend.

Step 2

Tape the photograph down to a table top or to a clipboard. Tape a piece of tracing paper or velum over the photograph. Allow the bottom to remain unattached, so you can insert a white piece of paper under the tracing paper.

This will enable you to check your progress.

Step 3

Using the Burnt Ochre Prisma Color pencil, begin to trace the face. Outline the general features and the areas that you know won't change, such as the eyes, the nostrils, the edge of the face, the clothes, and any general shadows that may be present in the photo. The main focus is to get the general shape and capture the key features so we don't lose them during the next step. Continually check your progress by inserting the white paper between your tracing and photograph.

Step 4

Still using the Burnt Ochre Prisma Color pencil, start to establish the shadows, using the side of the pencil to begin adding the basic shadows. Start to add the pencil lines for the hair. Next use a dark brown color to add depth to the shadows. This will create a bit of dimension to our newly created shadows.

Step 5

At this point, return to the Burnt Ochre Prisma Color and add age lines. Pay particular attention to creating sharp edges of shadow in each crease or wrinkle, blending them upward. Also create all the larger folds and depressions. Remember, pressing harder on the pencil and going over the same area again and again will make those areas darker and allow you to blend and create roundness.

Step 6

First use Dark Umber Prisma Color pencil and add those much-needed dark areas, such as the nostrils, the eyes, etc. Use the same pencil and sharpen the wrinkle lines and further depress the shadows.

The Beige Prisma Color pencil is next, adding a nice even tone to the whole drawing and beginning to soften the shadows. Preliminary highlights are added with the Cream Prisma Color pencil.

Step 7

Peach Prisma Color can be used to help add a subtle redness to the darker areas. Light Peach Prisma Color is used to add the same subtle redness to the highlighted areas.

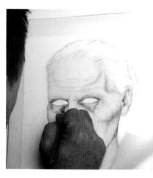

Step 8

Next, refine all the lines and wrinkles by darkening every color, every highlight and every shadow. Re-draw with each color to help accentuate and soften. Color is also added at this point, green in the eyes and red to the lips. Begin to put shadows into the hair. A White Prisma Color pencil and Light Peach Prisma Color pencil can be used to soften some of the colors; these are utilized to blend the other colors together.

Step 9

Using black as the main shadow for the hair and grey as an accent, create an older style to match the make-up we are planning. Since we have aged the model quite a bit, we have chosen a whitish grey color for the hair. Black is used to indicate the shadows between the hairs.

Step 10

Add more flesh tones to the overall drawing; specifically, add a Peach Prisma Color into the cheek, chin, nose and forehead. Gray, black and dark brown are added into the hair and eyes, as well as lashes. A little dark gray was added into the darkest shadows to further deepen them.

Step 11

Using the light brown to soften some of the shadows. Lightly blend the light brown into the surrounding skin area. This will help some of the darker shadows to blend a little bit better.

Step 12

Finally, capillaries are added to the nose, chin, and cheeks. Red was also added into the eyes. Light Umber Prisma Color pencil was used to create the age spots on the forehead and cheeks. A Teal pencil was used to create the veins. Use the Terra Cotta Prisma Color pencil to create surface redness. As a final touch, the clothes were quickly colored to finish the look of the drawing.

You have the choice of presenting the finished drawing with the original picture underneath it or side by side with the original drawing. Either way will allow the production staff to see exactly what you are intending to do with the make-up.

The finished drawing should first and foremost look like the performer. Secondly, it should be aged to the desired age range. Based on your drawing, the production company will have a clear understanding of what the actor will look like in the make-up.

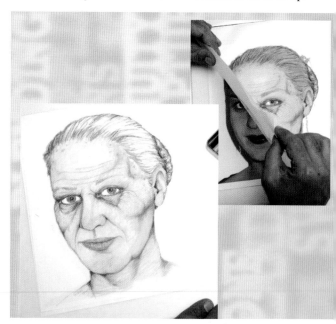

Aging Stipple

This technique was first used in the original "Mummy" to make the actor appear really old. Since then it has been used on numerous films to create a variety of ages. The most notable examples were on Jessica Tandy in "Driving Miss Daisy" and on Gloria Stuart in "Titanic". Both these films were nominated for an academy award and one of them won. The other similarity to these two films are both actresses were in their eighties; the point is, this technique works very well in creating wrinkles on older skin - so well in two examples, the films were nominated for an academy award for make-up; therefore, use this technique if your performer is older and has very pliable skin and the desired age you are trying to create includes wrinkles. If you are trying to age someone to fifty, this technique is not the best choice, although it can be combined with prosthetics or with simple highlight and shadow to create other effects. On Gloria Stuart in "Titanic," the make-up was very subtle, a combination of highlight, shadow and aging stipple being used to believably age her to one hundred and one.

> **There are five very simple steps that must be followed exactly or the technique will not work:**
>
> *1. Stretch the skin*
> *2. Apply the latex*
> *3. Dry the latex*
> *4. Powder the latex*
> *5. Release the skin*

Step 1

The model for Aging Stipple. In this example we will apply the latex around the eye to age that area. Rarely will you do the whole face, but usually only small areas in conjunction with a prosthetic appliance or Paint and Powder Make-up.

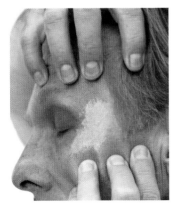

Step 2

Stretching the skin of the eye to create horizontal wrinkles, and applying latex over the stretched skin. Latex is a contact adhesive, so if you let the latex dry on the sponge and on the skin, touching the two together they will bond and you will be left with a sponge glued to your actor's face.

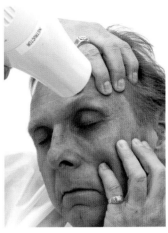

Step 3

Apply the latex in very thin layers. Several thin layers of latex are better than one thick layer. Usually you will apply 2 layers, one right after the other. Make sure you keep the edges thin and blended into the skin. Use a blow-dryer to completely dry the latex. Continue to hold the skin in position as you dry the latex.

Step 4

Apply powder over the dried latex with a powder puff. This will keep the latex from sticking to itself. Now you can release the skin.

Step 5

The model is helping by stretching the lower eye lid area. The lower eye is pulled down in three different directions. We are trying to achieve a curved wrinkle under the eye. So we pull down across the nose, straight down from the eye, and down across the cheek bone. Two layers of latex are applied to the area; again a cotton swab can be used to get in close to the lower lashes.

Step 6

For the larger area under the eye, we suggest using a sponge. Again being careful of any dry areas of latex, and make sure you are blending the overlapping areas of latex. You do not want to leave any space between each area of latex.

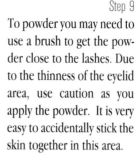

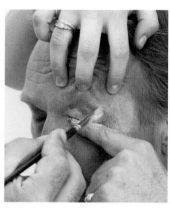

Step 9

To powder you may need to use a brush to get the powder close to the lashes. Due to the thinness of the eyelid area, use caution as you apply the powder. It is very easy to accidentally stick the skin together in this area.

Step 10

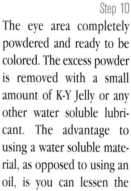

The eye area completely powdered and ready to be colored. The excess powder is removed with a small amount of K-Y Jelly or any other water soluble lubricant. The advantage to using a water soluble material, as opposed to using an oil, is you can lessen the amount of material with water.

Step 7

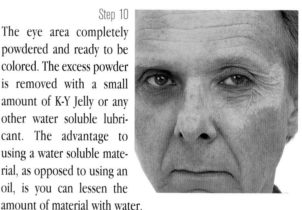

As previously, dry the latex then powder it. The performer can now open his eye without it sticking open.

Step 11

Adding subtle color to the eye. Rubber Mask grease paint must be used to color latex. The latex will absorb the vehicle in regular types of make-up, causing the make-up to discolor on the surface of the latex. When you color this type of make-up application you only do

the general highlights and shadows, the flesh tones, and colors like red and green.

Step 8

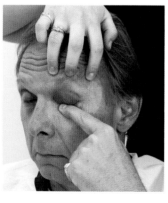

Stretching the eyelid area and applying latex on it. The model is helping to hold the lid down as the eyebrow is pulled up, a cotton swab works better to get in close to the performers lashes.

The finished effect on the left eye. By only doing the eye area illustrates how you can incorporate paint and powder make-up with the aging stipple.

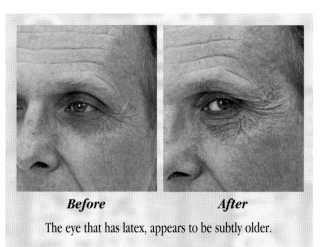

Before   **After**

The eye that has latex, appears to be subtly older.

It cannot be stressed enough that if you do not do this in the right order you will have a mess. When stretching the skin always keep in mind which way you want the wrinkles to run. To achieve horizontal wrinkles you will stretch the skin vertically, and for vertical wrinkles the skin should be streched horizontally.

To do this process on the entire face, begin at the neck and work your way up. Remember, if you only want to do certain areas you can start anywhere you want. The following will explain how to stretch all the areas of the face. You can then follow through by doing the five steps outlined above. To do the neck, have the performer look up as you pull down on his chest. This will create a horizontal wrinkle on the neck. Along the jaw line back to the ear, place your hand on the performer's ear, your other hand on the chin, and stretch the skin horizontally, creating a vertical wrinkle over the cheek. The rest of the cheek and the nasal labial fold area is next. Have the performer pull his mouth down and away from the nasolabial fold while you pull up and out on the cheek bone. For the lips and chin, placing a finger on each side of the performer's mouth, stretch apart. The eyes have to be done in three parts, the first being the crows' feet; pull down on the performer's cheek and up on the temple area. For the upper lid, have the performer hold his lashes down while you lift up on the eyebrows. (The under eye area is the trickiest.) Have the performer pull his nose down and away from the eye as you pull down on the cheek and pull down and away on the outside cheek area. For the forehead, pull down on the eyebrows as you hold hairline in place.

Even though you could do the whole face this way it should not necessarily be done unless your character absolutely needs it. This is a time-consuming process which only creates one type of effect.

Coloring this make-up must be done with rubber mask grease paint because it is rubber. However, washes of color are recommended as opposed to opaque applications. The latex is very translucent and you could get it to blend by simply using a small amount of K-Y Jelly over it.

Finally, we will comment briefly about how well this make-up will hold up. For the most part using just latex will create a fairly strong durable make-up, but if you want the make-up to be a little stronger, especially around the mouth, make the first layer Pros-aide adhesive. Also, the more layers of latex you use the more wrinkles you will create. Be careful, too many layers of latex and you will have a monster.

Notes:

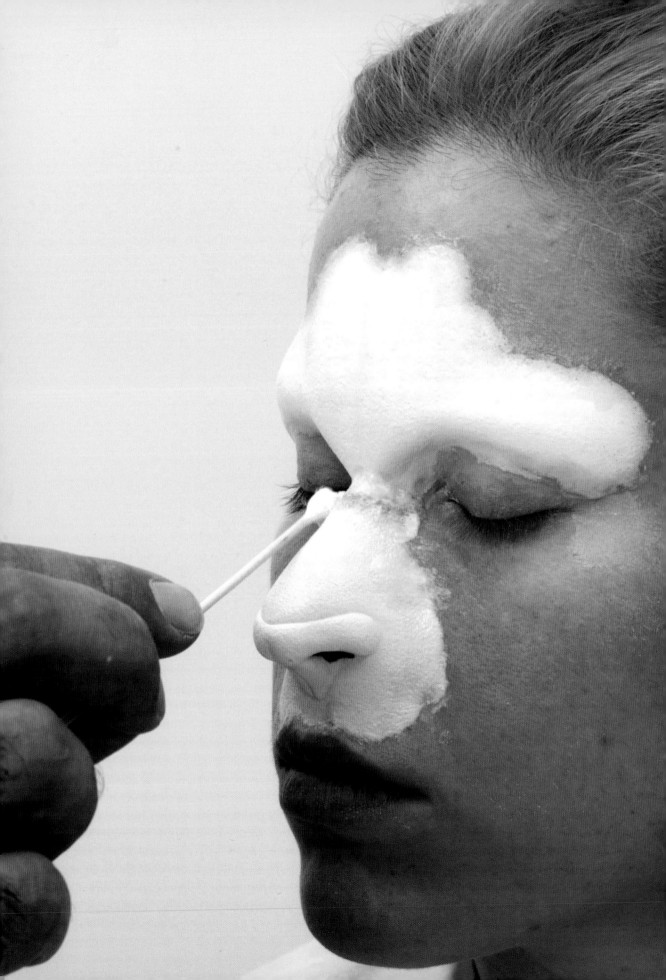

Chapter 4

Prosthetic Appliances

In the following chapters we will focus on how to make prosthetic appliances, from taking a life cast to using the variety of materials used for the appliances themselves. This is an introduction to prosthetic appliances and their use. We could write an entire book on this subject, but instead will give you a comprehensive look at how the appliances are made and the application of the different types of materials available to you.

Introduction to Prosthetics

Foam latex has been the staple material for prosthetic appliances since its first use. In recent years, there has been a push for more realistic materials, such as gelatin and silicone. However, several artists continue to use foam with stunning success.

Before we explain how to put on a prosthetic appliance, we should first talk about how a prosthetic is made. Production tends to believe prosthetics magically appear on set. It is our responsibility, the make-up artist, to educate production as to how or what it requires to produce a prosthetic appliance. It is very important for you to understand and be able to explain the process to production.

With so many choices out there, how do we decide which material is best. Each material has advantages and disadvantages. There are six different materials, latex, foam latex, gelatin, silicone GFA (gel filled appliances), foamed gelatin, and poly-urethane foam.

Latex is used primarily in the Halloween industry and sometimes on stage. It is poured into a mold and allowed to dry. Latex appliances are very simple to make and are extremely durable, however, late does not move well and may be hard to blend into the surrounding skin.

Foam latex is the most common material used today. It is light, soft, extremely flexible, and compresses well. It is completely opaque, meaning you cannot see through it. This type of appliance is best suited for make-ups where you do not need the actor's skin tone to show through. It is also the best choice for large or thick prosthetic appliances. Foam latex prosthetic appliances are the most durable, especially if you are doing a green

monster and translucency is not an issue.

Gelatin is used mainly for small appliances such as injuries. It is translucent and flexible, however it does not compress well. Its translucency is its best trait. A nice feature of gelatin is the edges can be dissolved with witch hazel. Gelatin is very easy to apply and color, so for small applications it is ideal, even if you have to apply it twice in one day.

Silicone GFA is one of the most realistic feeling prosthetic appliances you will ever encounter. It is silicone gel covered with a urethane skin. The top of the appliance, or the outer skin of it, moves independently of the skin attached to the actor's face. This gives the appliance very believable movement; also it is a very translucent appliance. This type of appliance seems to work best when thin. Some artists have stated they prefer to apply this appliance as one piece, as opposed to doing a multi-piece prosthetic make-up. We have found applying one piece is faster, however, working with multiple pieces is no different than working in any other material.

Foam gelatin is very similar to gelatin appliances. It is translucent, but not as transparent as regular gelatin. However, the big difference between gelatin and foam gelatin is the movement. Foam gelatin compresses well, so it moves better than regular gelatin. Because of the weight of the gelatin this type of prosthetic is best used thin.

Poly-urethane appliances are mostly used in Europe for stage productions, and rarely used on film due to their lack of movement; they are best used for an area with little or no movement, like a bone protruding from a leg or maybe a nose. The softest poly-urethane foam is still harder than foam latex.

An experienced artist can of course make any one of the six materials look good. We have tried to break them down into simple categories; it is now up to you to play and experiment with each one.

Making foam latex appliances, or any other appliances for that matter, is usually done the same way. First, a life cast is done of the performer, then a sculpture in oil-based clay is made of the desired piece. A negative mold is then made of the sculpture. The clay is removed from the molds and thoroughly cleaned. Foam latex is then injected into the space in the molds left by the clay. The foam is then cooked for several hours. After the foam is cooked, the mold is opened and a foam latex prosthetic appliance is removed. This appliance is a custom-made piece designed to fit the person originally cast. Although that was an overly simplified description of how to make a prosthetic appliance, it is easy to see why a custom piece of this nature can be very expensive. Once the molds are made, many pieces can be produced from them, enabling us to maintain the continuity of the make-up each time it is applied, particularly as each piece can only be used once. The following chapters will cover the making of the different prosthetic appliances more thoroughly, as well as how they are applied.

Notes:

Chapter 5

Foam Latex Prosthetics

Prosthetic appliances is a very diverse subject. In this book we are not trying to educate you on every aspect of making a prosthetic appliance. Rather, we are going to focus on the application of prosthetic appliances. In order for you to speak intelligently to production about this subject and its many aspects, you should have a general overview, a step-by-step look at what it takes to make an appliance for a project.

The following is a step-by-step procedure on how to create a prosthetic appliance.

Life Casting
The first step in creating a prosthetic make-up.

Step 1
Prepping the model for the life casting process. A plastic drape is used to protect the performer's clothing. Duct tape is carefully applied to keep the Alginate from flowing under the drape. The performer's hair is slicked back and ready for a bald cap. If the performer had long hair you would simply run the hair down the middle of the back.

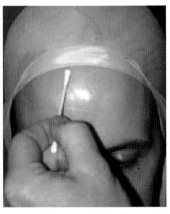

Step 2
A vinyl or a latex bald cap is used to cover the performer's hair. Pros-aide adhesive is used to glue the cap to the performer. First, slip the cap on making sure it is positioned properly. Apply the adhesive to the skin and to the cap and allow both surfaces to dry completely. Pros-aide is a contact adhesive and, by allowing both surfaces to dry, and then pressing them together, a permanent bond will be created.

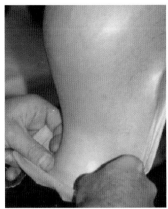

Step 3
Apply the back of the cap. Again, using Pros-aide adhesive, apply glue to the back of the neck and to the inside of the cap. Let both surfaces dry, then, with the performer tipping his head back, pull the cap down then forward into the adhesive. If the performer's hair is long and you have allowed it to hang down onto the back, then you will need to apply the adhesive on each side of the ponytail. Remember, it is very important to get the back of the neck to be as flat as possible.

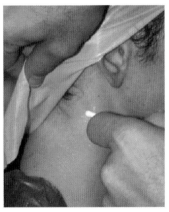

Step 4
Now apply the adhesive along the hairline starting at the back anchoring point and working your way up to the ear, again applying the adhesive to both the skin and the cap. If you need the ear as part of your cast then you would cut the ear out before completing this step. (To learn how to cut out the ear for a bald cap see chapter 5) Next, apply adhesive from the ear to the front anchor point. Attach the entire side before moving to the other side of the head.

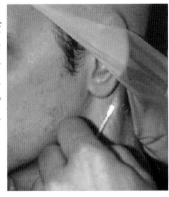

Step 5
Move to the other side of the head and repeat the same steps as before, applying adhesive to the skin and to the cap, allowing both to dry, then pressing them together.

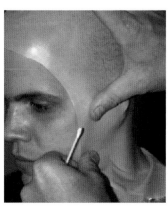

Step 6

Complete this side by applying adhesive from the ear to the front anchor point. Try to keep the adhesive close to the hairline, allowing for as much of the performer's skin that is exposed.

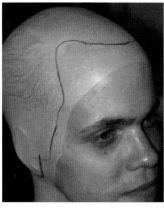

Step 7

Use a grease pencil to mark the hairline. If you are creating a character that is wearing a bald cap, or you know the prosthetic will not be anywhere near the performers hairline, you may omit this step. This line will be transferred to the alginate and then to your positive mold, letting you know exactly where your performer's hairline is located.

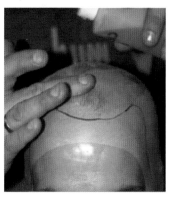

Step 8

We have found, in some cases, the bald cap can stick to the alginate, which may translate onto a torn or ruined life cast. To alleviate this problem simply apply castor oil or Vaseline to the cap. The eyebrows and eyelashes should also be coated to keep them from being pulled when you take the cast off.

Step 9

In two separate bowls, prepare your alginate and water. The water should be a little warm to the touch. The type of alginate will dictate what the water temperature should be. The alginate we are using is a prosthetic grade cream. If you are attempting this process with dental alginate then you will need cooler water. Alginate is a very simple material to adjust. The colder the water, the longer your working time; the warmer the water, the shorter the working time. It is that simple. If you are using prosthetic grade cream then you have about 7 minutes of working time. If you are using dental alginate your working time will be dramatically decreased, down to about a minute and a half. Pour the water into the alginate while you slowly start to stir the mixture with your hand.

Step 10

Continue to stir until achieving a smooth creamy consistency, making sure there are no chunks of unmixed alginate.

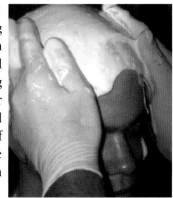

Step 11

With the performer sitting in an upright position, with eyes closed, place the bowl of alginate in his lap asking him to hold it in place for you; now carefully spread the alginate over the top of his head, making sure the alginate is going on smooth and even.

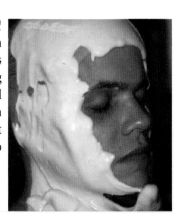

Step 12

Work the alginate down each side of the performer's face, using large sweeping motions. Pick up a handful of alginate as you do each side being very careful not to apply the alginate too thinly.

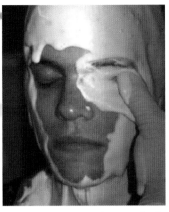

Step 13

Work your thumb into each eye area, covering the eye with the alginate. By placing the alginate into the eye area in this fashion you will help alleviate any air bubbles in the corners of the eyes. Repeat the same procedure for the other eye. Work the material first across the eyes then cover the mouth. Leaving the nose for last, use your finger tips to pat the alginate over the top of the nose.

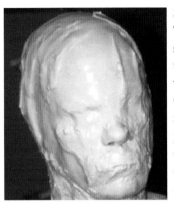

Step 14

There is no need for any straws or breathing tubes in the nose or mouth. Simply work quickly and carefully. Once everything is covered allow the alginate to completely set up. Depending on how fast you work will depend how much time is left.

Step 15

Prepare the plaster bandages by tearing them into two different lengths, with one pile large, the other small. The specific size is based on the size of the cast as well as what you may be used to working with. For a facial cast prepare about four rolls of bandages. Fill a bowl about half full with hot water and place on your model's lap. The warmer the water the faster the plaster bandages will set. Fast setting plaster bandages are available too.

Step 16

Pick up three bandages of the same length, at one time, and dip the prepared plaster bandages into the water, wringing out the excess water. By applying three layers at a time you will be able to build up a good strong thickness from the beginning. Start at the top of the head and work down.

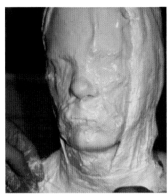

Step 17

Once the first piece is applied to the top of the head, run the ends as far down the side of the head as possible. Apply your next pieces over the first piece and run them down to the neck, creating a nice perimeter. Starting at the neck area now work up, laying your pieces horizontally and overlapping each prior piece.

Step 18

Cover the entire face area with these horizontal pieces of bandage. Because each layer is three bandages thick and is overlapping the previous layer, the entire cast is a uniform six layers thick. When working around the nose make sure you leave a space for the nostrils. You don't want to cover up the nostrils, that would be bad. Take two small pieces of bandage and roll them into a small piece that can be applied between the nostrils to give that area strength. If you are at all unsure of the strength of that area of the cast add more bandages. This area needs to be the strongest.

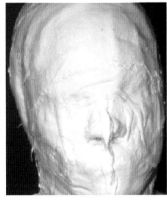

Step 19

Let the cast cure for about five minutes or until it is hard to the touch. Do not knock on the cast. Take this opportunity to clean up some of your materials and to start to clean up your model.

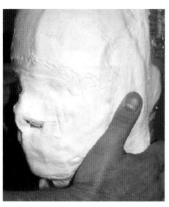

Step 20

To remove the cast have the model flex facial muscles, while slowly exhaling through the mouth. Grip each side of the cast and gently pull, slowly working it off the face. Be careful, the cast may stick slightly to the bald cap or any exposed hair, so go slow.

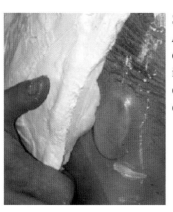

Step 21

Another way to remove the cast is to simply hold on to it firmly, allowing the model to slowly pull his face out.

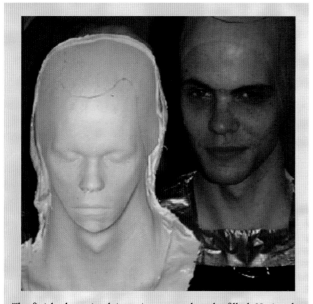

The finished cast in alginate is now ready to be filled. Notice the cast appears to be a positive image of the performer, but in reality it is a negative impression of his face.

The Positive Mold

The positive mold will be an exact copy of the actor in cement.

Step 1

The alginate cast needs to be filled right after its removal from the performer, or it will shrink, defeating the whole purpose of casting the actor in the first place. Ultracal 30 is the stone material we will use to fill the mold. Either hemp or burlap cut into strips can be used for reinforcing this mold. Reinforcing material is essential to creating a strong mold that will last a long time.

Step 2

Fill a large bowl one third full of warm water, slowly sifting in small amounts of Ultracal 30. Coat the surface then allow the cement to sink. Sprinkle in more cement until the material stops sinking. You will know when you have added enough cement to the water because the cement will stop sinking and will absorb the water, forming a dried lake bed appearance in the bowl. Allow to stand for a moment, then mix together. A jiffy mixer can be used, but beware, the jiffy mixer will cause the cement to set up faster. In most cases your hand will work best to thoroughly mix the cement.

Step 3

Use a small brush to carefully paint in the ultracal over the entire surface of the alginate. This first layer is called the splash coat. The first layer got its name from an old technique in which the artist used to splash the cement into a mold or over a sculpture. Be very careful not to trap air bubbles in the cement as you paint over the alginate.

Step 4

As the Ultracal thickens build up a thickness of about half an inch. Work slowly making sure the cement is a uniform thickness. The vertical surfaces are the hardest area to build up to the desired thickness.

Slowly scoop cement from the bottom of your mold and move it to the sides. Repeat this step until the cement stops sliding down. Allow this first layer to set but not cure.

Step 5

Once the first layer is set mix up another batch of Ultracal-30. This batch is for our reinforcement layer. Either burlap cut into strips or hemp balled up into a nest can be utilized. Dip the hemp or the burlap into the bucket of cement and wring out the excess cement. Apply the cement soaked fibers all over the surface of the mold. Add a second layer of fibers all around the edge of the mold to strengthen the edge.

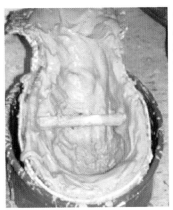

Step 6

A wooden handle can be inserted into the mold at this point. Wrap the ends of the handle with burlap or hemp for added strength. Mix a third and final batch of Ultracal 30. This batch will be our beauty coat. Just as the name implies, this is where you make the mold pretty. Mix up this batch a little thicker than the previous batches. Apply it with a spatula, a kidney tool, or your fingers. Fill in all low areas and flatten any sharp areas.

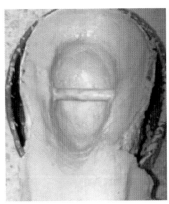

Step 7

Use a small amount of water on a sponge or with a rubber kidney tool. Smooth out the surface as the mold cures. As the cement cures it will heat up and the cement will quickly become un-workable – so work fast.

Step 8

Allow the Ultracal-30 to completely cure, then pull the cast out of the alginate negative mold. The cast is now ready to be cleaned up. The alginate mold should be discarded. If this mold was made of a silicone life-casting cream then the mold could be saved and other casts could be made from it. Alginate will shrink as it dries out, so the longer you have the smaller it will get.

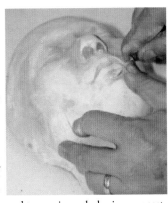

Step 9

The cast needs to be cleaned of all sharp edges, air bubbles, and any other imperfections. Use a sharp tool and carefully knock off any raised areas. A hand plainer can be used to round off the edges and smooth out the corners of the cast. You may need to mix up a small amount of ultracal to repair any holes in your cast.

Step 10

As soon the cast is cleaned up, apply a coat of castor oil over it. This will help the cast to last. The Ultracal continues to dry out and lose moisture. The castor oil will replace that moisture, and will not affect the foam latex that will be run in it later.

Sculpting

Clay is used to create the look of our prosthetic appliance.

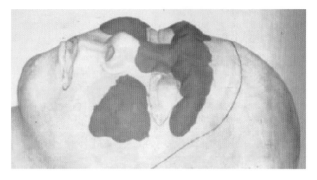

Step 1

The cast is now ready for clay. Roma plastalina is typically used to sculpt prosthetic appliances. However, some materials such as silicone have an adverse reaction to the sulfur in the clay. Chavant clay is becoming a popular choice for a sulfur free clay as it seemingly appears to be more consistent than the Roma Plastalina. The first step to sculpting a prosthetic appliance is to rough out the sculpture. Do this by applying small pieces of softened clay to the surface of the cast. The cast is representing the performer's face with small pieces of clay applied to alter his features. Do not worry about detail at this point. You want to simply build up a rough version of the sculpture.

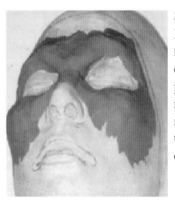

Step 2

Focus on symmetry and getting the proper look of the character. Smooth the small pieces together only to make sure there are no gaps in the clay. The focus is not to smooth the whole thing out.

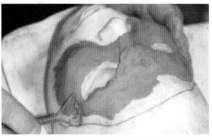

Step 3

Once the sculpture is the proper shape it is ready to be raked. Using different sizes of rakes, begin to smooth down the clay. The rake is a sculpting tool with many small teeth.

Use the largest rake first, working down in size till you are using a very fine rake. The teeth of the rake drag across the clay removing the high spots and filling the low spots (crisscrossing this tool really starts to smooth out the sculpt). Raking over the edge of the clay helps to create a fine blended edge, but be careful not to scratch the surface of the cast.

Step 4

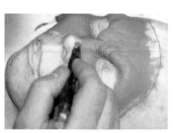

Now that the shape is really taking form you can start to create wrinkles and texture. Carve in your heavy wrinkles first, then your smaller wrinkles; each time use a couple of rakes to smooth out the wrinkles, giving them realistic roundness. Small bits of clay can be added here and there to create veins and also to add fullness or roundness to an area. A rubber tool can be used to further blend the edge. A small amount of 99% alcohol or acetone can also be used to smooth out and around the wrinkles and skin texture.

Step 5

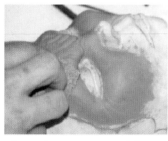

Texture the whole sculpture with a small sponge or a texture pad. Be careful not to squash or distort any detail, this is just the preliminary texture. With a small wire loop tool make faint skin texture lines in the clay, making sure you are following the actual skin lines. Follow the lines in the performer's skin, that are present on the cast, carrying them onto the clay. Next take the same loop tool and lightly create directional pores on the surface of the clay over the lines you have just made. Use a light tapping method and allow the pores to appear random.

Step 6

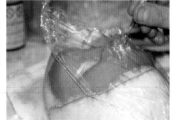

Clear plastic can also be draped over the sculpture to create faint lines and subtle textures.

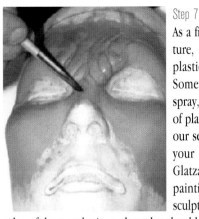

Step 7

As a final step to our sculpture, paint on a layer of plastic film as a sealer. Some artists use a clear spray, but we use a mixture of plastic and plasticizer for our sealer; you could make your own by thinning Glatzan in acetone and painting that over your sculpture. Never paint the edge of the prosthetic, as that edge should be as thin as possible.

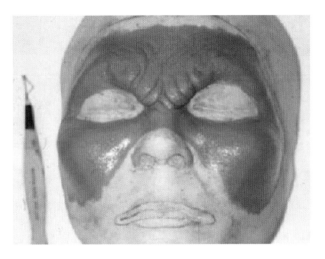

The finished sculpture is now ready for the next step.

The Negative Mold

Molding the sculpture so that the prosthetic appliance can be repeatedly run in foam latex.

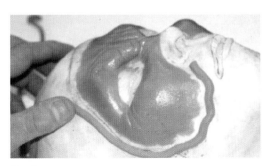

Step 1

With a clay extruder lay out a triangular clay extrusion. Lay the clay all around your sculpture about quarter of an inch from the sculpture. This will be the front edge of our retaining wall. Be careful not to touch the sculpture with this wall.

Step 2

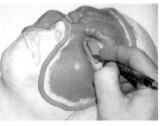

All large areas of exposed cement need to be covered with clay, even the eyelids. Again, do not touch the sculpture with the clay. Lay a pad of clay over the eyelid then cut around the pad creating a clean 90 degree angle from the cement.

Step 3

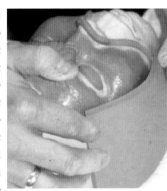

Water based clay, also known as white clay, can be used over the rest of the cast. Since we are only making a mold of the sculpture area we do not have to worry about the detail on the rest of the cast. Also, if you didn't cover the cast with clay you would have a problem with de-molding the two halves or possibly never get the mold apart.

Step 4

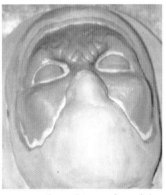

The water based clay is laid over the rest of the cast and then flared out at the bottom. Two square holes are cut into the clay and removed, leaving bare cement as touch points for the mold. (This will help the molds fit better.) Notice the exposed cement all around the sculpture; it is important to keep this area free of clay or any debris.

Step 5

Mix up small amount of Ultracal 30. This will be our splash coat. Place water in the bowl and slowly sift in cement until you have achieved a dried lake bed effect. Let it stand for a moment then mix thoroughly.

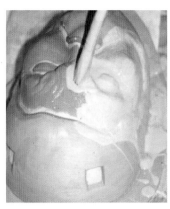

Step 6

Slowly and carefully brush the splash coat over the entire sculpture, making sure you are not trapping any air bubbles against the surface and being careful not to damage the sculpture itself. Once the sculpture is covered you can now work over the rest of the clay area

Step 7

Work the splash coat over the mold, covering every area. Now build a little thickness by applying more cement over the first layer. Once you have built up a thickness of a quarter of an inch allow the cement to slightly set. It should be stiff but not hard.

Step 8

Mix up a new batch of Ultracal 30 for the reinforcement layer, using either burlap or hemp as the reinforcement. Dip the burlap into the new mixture of cement and wring out the excess cement. Apply the cement soaked burlap over the entire mold, working out any air bubbles as you go. If you use hemp, you will only need one layer. If you use burlap, you will need two overlapping layers.

Step 9

Mix up a third batch of cement, this will be the beauty coat. This third batch should be just a little thicker than the previous two. Once it is thoroughly mixed, apply to the mold using a rubber kidney tool, a spatula, or your hand. Create a flat top to the mold so it will not rock when laid

open. This top layer should be smoothed as it is applied in order to achieve a nice even surface.

Step 10

Let the mold completely cure then turn over. Remove all the exposed clay. A plainer can be used to round any sharp edges.

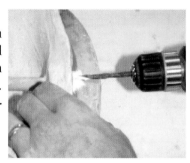

Step 11

To remove the cast from the negative mold drill two small holes, one on each side of the cast. This will allow a screwdriver into the cast.

Step 12

Using two screwdrivers simultaneously gently pry the cast out of the negative mold. Slow gentle pressure is better than one hard push on the screwdrivers. As soon as the cast moves, slowly pull it free of the negative mold.

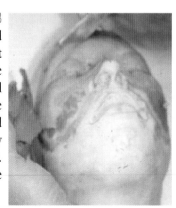

Step 13

Clean all the clay off and out of each mold. Do not use metal tools to remove the clay since they will scratch the surface of the mold. A wooden tool used very carefully will work very well to remove all the clay. Both molds need to be completely clean.

Foam Latex

Once all the mold pieces are clean the mold can be plumbed with extrusion holes and filled with foam latex or any other prosthetic material.

Step 1

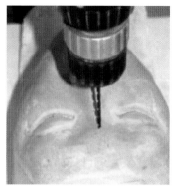

To get the foam latex into the mold, drill an injection hole in the positive mold. Center the hole in the middle of the area of the prosthetic. The hole should be located in a thick area of the sculpture. The foam latex will flow into the mold a bit easier if there is room under the injection hole. Drill this small hole all the way through the cast.

Step 2

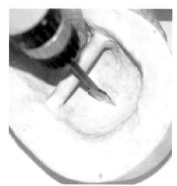

Turn the cast over and drill a larger hole using the smaller drill hole as a guide. This hole should be the same size as the nozzle of your injector gun. Only drill this hole half way through the cast.

Step 3

A small piece of PVC pipe can be glued into the hole to make the fit between the injector gun and the mold a little tighter or to elevate the injector hole, making it more accessible.

Step 4

Preparing the foam latex. Follow the directions that come with the foam latex kit; each manufacturer provides different formulas for their particular foams. You will need a gram scale to weigh out the various components. (The room must be cool, with low humidity.) The first is the foam latex base. Pour into a large bowl, following the manufacturer's directions for its size and the type of mixer you will be using. We are using a Sunbeam Mixmaster to mix the foam and are using the large bowl formula.

Step 5

Foaming agent is the next ingredient to be poured into the bowl. (The foaming agent is a soap product that causes the latex to foam up.) Now, pour the curing agent into the same bowl. This product is the third component in our four component foam latex kit. The Curing agent will help .

Step 6

Gelling agent is poured into a small separate cup and set aside. The Gelling agent will be added last and will cause the foamed latex to gel.

Step 7

Place the large bowl into the mixer and place the mixer on a low speed to combine all the chemicals. Most directions suggest just one minute to do this. It is critical you follow a strict schedule. A digital timer is perfect to keep accurate time. Next, turn the mixer to a high speed, whipping air into the foam mixture. Once the proper volume is achieved slow the mixer down to refine the foam. This will make the bubbles in the foam latex a uniform size. Further, slow down the mixer; this will ultra refine the foam latex.

Step 8

Slowly add the Gelling agent into the mixture over a thirty second period while the mixer remains at its low speed. After the Gelling agent is added, use a spatula and turn the bowl in the opposite direction to ensure the Gelling agent is thoroughly mixed in.

Step 9

Pour the entire mixture into an injection gun. Hold the injection gun at a 45 degree angle as you pour in the foam; be careful not to trap air at the end of the gun.

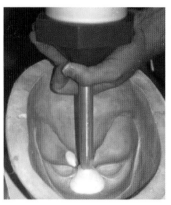

Step 10

You can either inject the foam latex into an open faced mold, as seen here, or into the injection holes seen in Step 12.

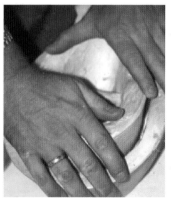

Step 11

After you fill the opened mold with foam, slowly lower the positive side of the mold into the filled negative. The excess will squeeze out the sides of the molds. Apply gentle pressure to insure a snug fit, which translates into thin edges.

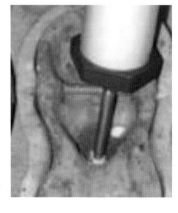

Step 12

Injecting a mold that is already closed. The injection gun fits snugly to the injector hole. The trapped air and excess foam will extrude out of the extrusion holes.

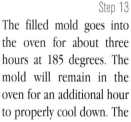

Step 13

The filled mold goes into the oven for about three hours at 185 degrees. The mold will remain in the oven for an additional hour to properly cool down. The oven circulates heated air around the mold. The heat can be turned off at the required time and the oven will still circulate the air around the mold, cooling it slowly.

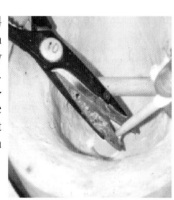

Step 14

The injector and extrusion foam can be cut away before opening the mold. Utilizing a sharp pair of scissors, gently pull on the extruded foam latex and cut away as much of the foam as possible.

Step 15

Using two screwdrivers, slowly pry the mold open. Slow gentle pressure is all that is needed to break the seal between the molds. You may rip the fragile appliance if you try to force the molds open too quickly.

Step 16

Carefully peel the mold halves apart. You may need to cut more of the extrusion with your scissors, or stick a finger into the mold, gently peeling the appliance from one half or the other.

Step 17

Powder the exposed side of the prosthetic appliance. Gently peel up the edge of the appliance, powdering as you go. Since the prosthetic is made of latex there is a chance it may stick to itself.

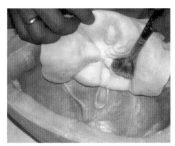

Step 18

Remove the flashing, the extruded foam around the prosthetic, and the prosthetic appliance, together, powdering as you go.

Step 3

Apply Pros-aide Adhesive to the inside center most point of the appliance. Then apply Pros-aide to the skin. Allow both to dry thoroughly. Press the two dried adhesive points together. This will form the anchoring point for the prosthetic. The Pros-aide is a contact adhesive that forms a strong bond when applied in this fashion.

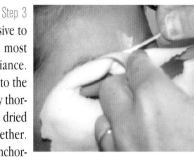

Application

This is the area on which we will be focusing most of our attention. The prosthetic appliance and all the tools necessary to apply it to the face.

Having a well organized station will aid in a faster application.

Step 4

The prosthetic appliance is glued down straight through the center of the appliance. This time do not wait for the adhesive to dry. Simply lift the prosthetic back to the anchor point and apply the adhesive to the skin. Leave the edges undone at this point. The Pros-aide can be used a variety of ways, either wet or completely dried. You can also apply the adhesive to both surfaces to be glued, or to just one surface. If you have a problem getting an area to stick you might want to apply the adhesive to both surfaces, allowing each area to dry completely, pressing them together, this process being the same as the anchor point, forming the strongest bond.

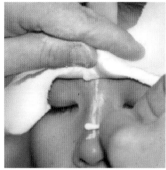

Step 1

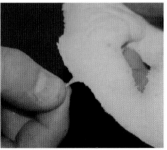

Before the prosthetic is applied to the face, you will need to remove the flashing and any injection or extrusion points. The edge also must be carefully checked for an over abundance of thin wispy foam. Do not tear off your thin edge, just remove the excess foam that is not necessary to blend the appliance.

Step 5

Hinge the prosthetic as if you are opening a door, then apply the adhesive to the skin. While it is still wet push the prosthetic into the glue.

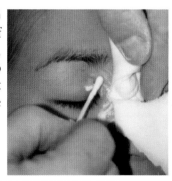

Step 2

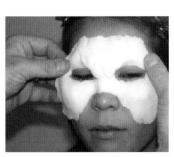

Test fit the prosthetic to the performer's face, making sure there is plenty of room for the eyes.

Step 6

Work back and forth from side to side. This will insure the prosthetic is going on straight.

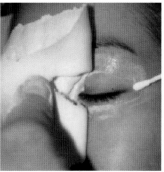

The performer should keep her eyes closed when you are working around the eye area. First, there is less chance you will get something in them and they will not accidently be glued open. As soon as the eye area is attached, powder the eyes, so the performer may open them again.

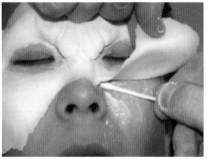

Step 8

The entire prosthetic must be completely glued down. The only area that might not be glued down is the eyebrow area.

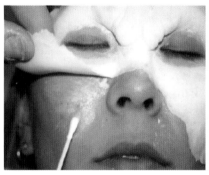

Step 9

The prosthetic only moves and wrinkles properly when it is glued everywhere. The prosthetic then becomes part of the face and moves very realistically.

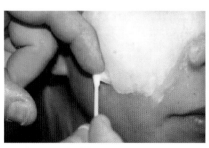

Step 10

The last area to be glued are the edges. Carefully apply adhesive under the thin edges, do not fold them over. If by accident you do fold an edge, then simply use a brush dampened with 99% alcohol. The alcohol causes the adhesive to lose its adhesion for a few seconds, allowing for the edge to be straightened. When the alcohol evaporates the edge sticks back to the skin, hopefully, straight and perfect.

Step 11

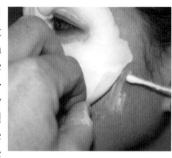

Another technique is to lift the edge and hold then apply the adhesive to the skin and allow it to completely dry. Then carefully lay the edge onto the dried glue and press down. The edges are now ready to be blended. Depending on how well you have applied the prosthetic and how thin the edges were in the first place will dictate how much blending you need to do to them now. If the edges are in good shape, then all you may need to do is apply a layer of Pros-aide over the edge to get it to blend properly. If the edge is a little thick you may wish to mix Cab-o-sil into your Pros-aide to create a thick paste we call Bondo. You will need to apply a layer of Pros-aide over the Bondo because the Bondo does not have any texture.

Step 12

Once the edges are blended you have a couple of color choices. For this application we chose Pax Paint as our base. Pax Paint is a mixture of three components. Mix 40% acrylic paint, 40% Pros-aide, and 20% matte medium. When making Pax Paint always mix your color before you add the Pros-aide. The Pros-aide is white in its liquid state but it drys clear.

Step 13

Apply the Pax Paint over the prosthetic appliance. The Pax Paint acts like a sealer for the appliance.

Step 14

Next, use rubber mask grease paint to blend the Pax Paint into the rest of the face.

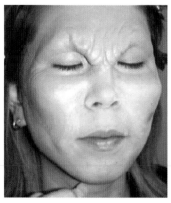

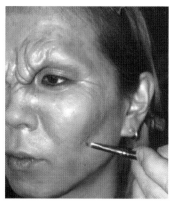

Step 15

Shadows and highlights are applied in rubber mask grease paint over the Pax Paint base.

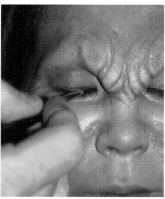

Step 16

Eye liner and wrinkles can be added to create texture and detail.

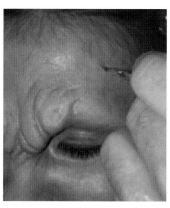

Step 17

Veins and capillaries are added to give the skin a translucent look.

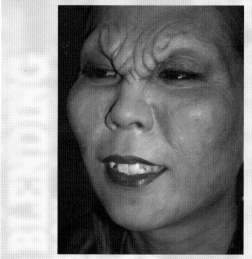

The finished make-up.

Foam Latex Prosthetic Application–Part 2

In this section we describe a second way to apply a Foam Latex Prosthetic. As with many of these techniques you have learned, there are multiple ways of doing the same type of make-up. The following is a very straight forward way of doing a foam latex application.

To apply the prosthetic appliance, first clean the model's face of any previous make-up or oils. To protect the wardrobe from the materials in the application, cover the model with a cover cloth, then apply Pros-Aide to skin at the center-most area of the appliance, allowing the Pros-Aide to completely dry. Press the appliance into the dried adhesive on skin. Because the Pros-Aide remains tacky, even after it is dry, it will hold the prosthetic in position but it is not so strong that you can easily lift and reposition if necessary. Lift each side of the prosthetic appliance and apply Pros-Aide under it. Allow the adhesive to dry, then press the piece into it. Continue in this fashion all the way around the piece, making sure every area of the appliance is glued down. The edge is the last area to secure. Lift the edge with tweezers and apply the adhesive under it. This time, while the glue is still wet, let the edge fall into it. If you accidently fold the delicate edge onto itself, use 99% alcohol to loosen the glue and smooth it out. Next, roll a cotton swab over the edge with more Pros-Aide on it to lay the edge into glue and smooth the edge.

Once everything is glued down use a cotton swab to stipple more Pros-Aide over edge to blend it. Again allow the Pros-Aide to completely dry. (A hair dryer will greatly speed up this process.) Dip a filbert brush into colorless powder, pressing it all the way around the edge of the appliance. Use a liberal amount of powder as this will help to fill in that subtle step from the appliance to the skin. Remove the excess powder with a brush that is dampened with 99% alcohol. At this point, it is easiest to see any edges that may be there for any variety of reasons. If there is an edge that is perceivable, a concoction of Pros-Aide and a chemical thickener called Cab-o-sil can be mixed together to create a smooth paste that is used to fill the gap between the skin and the edge of the appliance. This mixture is also known as Bondo. Pros-aid should be applied over the entire prosthetic to seal it and provide texture to the Bondo. (The Bondo usually is smooth and needs something over it to add texture.) Powder over the prosthetic so it will not stick to itself. The application of Pros-aide over the prosthetic will also help seal the prosthetic, and will keep the make-up from absorbing irregularly into the piece.

To color the prosthetic appliances, use Rubber Mask Grease Paint. The first color should be a shade of red, not a bright one but a subtle red such as one used to add redness to a face; apply a flesh tone that matches your performer - 99% alcohol is used to blend the make-up into the surrounding skin. Highlight and shadow the piece and add any accentuations that will be needed. A prosthetic grade make-up, like RMGP, must be used over a prosthetic appliance because of the nature of foam latex. Like latex, foam latex requires a castor oil based make-up that will not discolor or degrade the latex product. The colors you use in your application will be dictated by the type of prosthetic you are using.

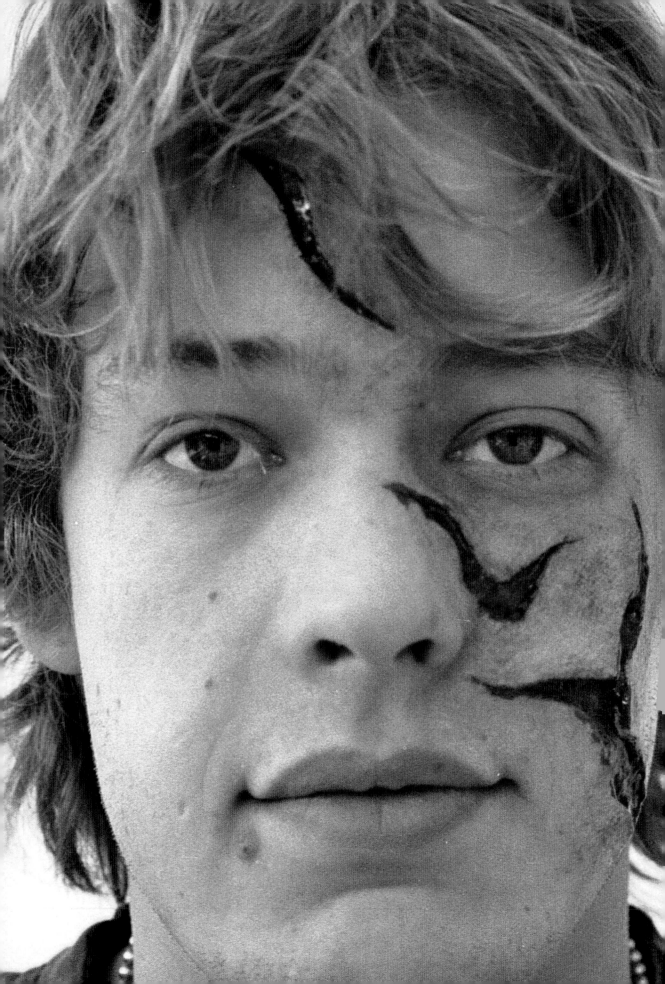

Chapter 6

Gelatin Prosthetics

Use Any Molds

Gel-Foam Cubex can be used to create just about any make-up effect you may dream up, but the formula is specifically designed to be poured into a mold. You, of course, can use existing foam latex molds or elect to make new ones.

Foam Gelatin Prosthetic

Gel-Foam Cubex is gelatin that has been whipped into a stable foam product. The process of foaming gelatin is still relatively new; however, Make-up Designory has developed and perfected a formula that is not only stable but also translucent and extremely soft. The Gel-Foam Cubex was developed with the end user in mind - for the purpose of creating a viable alternative to foam latex.

Gel-Foam Cubex cubes.

The following is a detailed description of how to use the Gel-Foam Cubex and the Gel-Foam Cubex Color Kit.

When making new models, keep in mind there is no need to bake the molds since the gelatin does not require baking. Unbaked molds will last longer than if they were used for foam latex. We have found cylinder style molds to be the best type of mold for gelatin. We typically use BJB's TC-1630 as our mold material. It has a good detail reproduction and holds up over time.

Large appliances can be used, however we found it better to use several small pieces as opposed to using one big piece.

The molds should be sprayed with a light coat of Epoxy Parafilm prior to filling with gelatin. Both the negative and the positive need to be sprayed.

Making the Appliance

Place the desired amount of Gel-Foam Cubex into a microwave safe bowl and heat on high in a microwave oven. Heat at one-minute intervals mixing in-between heating cycles. This is done so the flocking doesn't become scorched. Repeat this procedure until all lumps are removed. The gelatin is now ready to pour.
The Gel-Foam Cubex color kit can be used to tint or color the base cubes to any skin shade. The color kit comes with five colors, red, green, yellow, white, and brown. The color kit is made up of smaller cubes which can be torn off and added to the base cubes. Therefore, if your model is more olive than the base cubes it is easy to add a little yellow green to the mixture.

Pour the gelatin into the prepared mold, then close. Use a clamp to hold the mold tightly closed and to ensure thin edges in the prosthetic appliance.

The gelatin is ready to be de-molded in about 30 minutes. Carefully open the mold allowing the gelatin to stick to whichever side it wants to. Usually the gelatin will stick inside the negative side of the mold. The gelatin will remain fairly sticky so powder must be used to ensure the edges won't fold over and stick to themselves. Slowly peel the appliance out of the mold, powdering it as you go.

There is usually a small amount of excess gelatin around the edges of the prosthetic appliance, which we call the flashing. Leave only 1/8 of this flashing attached to the prosthetic, trimming the remainder away with scissors. The main reason for cutting the flashing is to reduce the weight and prevent tearing the delicate edges of the appliance. You should keep the flashing attached to the prosthetic appliance until you have the piece glued to the skin.

Gelatin Prosthetic Formula

This is standard formula if you want to make up your own gelatin prosthetic material. Several companies sell a pre-mixed formula of gelatin; all you have to do is melt and pour it into your mold. Ben Nye Company makes a product called Effects Gel, and Burman Industries make a version called Gel-effects.

Procedure

In a microwave safe bowl, mix 120 grams of sorbitol with 120 grams of glycerin. Slowly stir in 30 grams of gelatin crystals. In a separate container mix 33 grams of sorbitol with 3 grams of zinc oxide. With an eyedropper, add 9 drops of your zinc oxide/sorbitol mixture into the gelatin mixture. Stir in small amount of Rayon flocking until desired color is achieved. Stir well. Place into a microwave and cook on high for 1 minute, then remove and stir. Heat mixture once more for an additional minute and again remove and stir. Allow the gelatin to cool completely. Reheat mixture in microwave, slowly and on high one minute at a time. The total amount of time to completely heat up the mixture will vary. The gelatin is now ready to pour.

To ensure proper mixture allow the formula to completely cool and then re-heat. Doing this will help the gelatin to completely dissolve into the liquids.

To minimize air bubbles in your mixture we recommend placing the melted mixture into a vacuum chamber then de-gassing it.

The molds are made of BJB's TC-1630, a rigid casting urethane, and have been sprayed with Epoxy Parafilm as a release agent.

Pour the gelatin into the mold, then close. A clamp is used to ensure thin edges in the prosthetic.

De-mold in about 30 minutes.

Cylinder Molds For Gelatin Appliances

A cylinder mold is a small mold, primarily used for little pieces. It can be used for either foam latex prosthetics or gelatin prosthetics; a sturdy mold capable of many runs. We have found gelatin works best in small pieces and the cylinder mold is ideal for clamping.

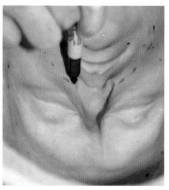

Step 1
The life cast process is the same as in the previous chapter. You have the choice of working directly from the alginate cast if you only need one piece or you can make the positive, as shown in the last chapter. We chose the latter, making a silicone negative of the positive, thus allowing us the ability to pull more than one positive out of the mold. In other words, we can make a positive of the chin and the eye areas and not have to worry about shrinkage or possibly damaging the alginate when we de-mold the first positive. We marked the area that we need with a black Sharpie pen.

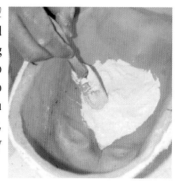

Step 2
Next, we mixed and brushed in a quick drying cement like Hydrocal into the mold. Make sure you go beyond your markings. You have to work very quickly, Hydrocal dries extremely fast.

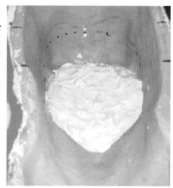

Step 3
Build up several layers of Hydrocal. You will need a good thickness to this mold piece. Allow the cement to completely cure.

Step 4
Carefully remove the new positive from the mold. Clean up any imperfections or surface bubbles.

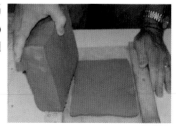

Step 5
Water based clay is cut into a uniform thickness and laid out on a board.

Step 6
Lay the Hydrocal positive onto the clay and cut away everything but one inch around the positive.

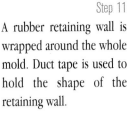

Step 11
A rubber retaining wall is wrapped around the whole mold. Duct tape is used to hold the shape of the retaining wall.

Step 7   Press the positive down firmly into the clay.

Step 8
Add another layer of clay on top of the clay slab. Sculpt the clay into the positive, creating a seamless transition from the positive to the clay.

Step 12
Leave about half an inch of space around the mold. This will allow the entire piece to be molded.

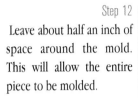

Step 13
Hot glue the rubber retaining wall to the board to keep the silicone from leaking out the bottom.

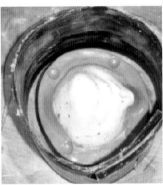

Step 9
Using a straight edge cut a clean straight line all around the clay.

Step 14
Mix up the silicone to its specifications and slowly pour the material over the newly sculpted mold. Pour slowly so you do not trap air against the surface of the mold.

Step 10
Cut four small circular depressions in the clay. These depressions will serve as the keys for the new mold.

Step 15
The silicone must completely cure before you move on. Once the silicone is cured, remove the retaining wall.

Step 16

Carefully peel the mold and the silicone off the board. You may need to use a wide spatula to break the seal from the board.

Step 17

Remove the clay and the Hydrocal positive from the silicone negative; (It may come out as one piece or may need to be removed a little bit at a time) completely clean the inside of any residue or debris.

Step 18

The new positive is going to be made of a castable urethane. You could use almost any material you are comfortable with. Since this mold will be used for gelatin and will never be baked, any fast drying cement could be used. The two choices we prefer are Ultracal-30 and TC-1630. The latter is the casting urethane we are using here.

Step 19

The urethane is a two part system that is measured into two equal parts, then mixed together. To ensure a thorough cure make sure the components are completely mixed before pouring.

Step 20

Pour the material into the silicone mold. The board can be vibrated to ensure all the air bubbles are forced to the surface.

Step 21

Fill the mold all the way to the top. Again, any material could be used for this mold.

Step 22

Once the urethane is fully cured, peel it out of the silicone negative. You now have a urethane positive that looks just like the Hydrocal and clay sculpture.

Step 23

Here are two examples of basically the same type of mold, one made of Ultracal-30 and the other, of TC-1630 urethane; both have sculptures on them and are sealed with a liquid plastic.

Step 24

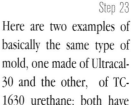

Both positives were pulled from the same life cast and were made in the same way. The final thing to do to the sculptures is texture them with an orange sponge.

Step 25

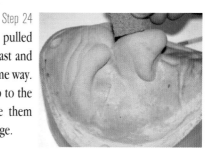

The chin also requires some texture. The clay used here is Roma Plastalina, which contains sulfur. Sulfur may cause a problem for some materials, like some silicones. Since we are using gelatin, the sulfur will not adversely affect it or its curing.

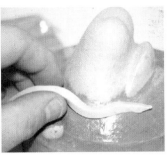

Step 26

A clay retaining wall is laid around the sculpture. Do not allow the clay wall to touch the sculpture.

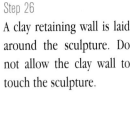

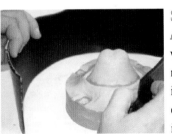

Step 27

The edge is laid out first then filled in with larger pieces of clay. In this example we used the same Roma Plastalina clay for the edge and then used a water based clay to fill in.

Step 28

A rubber retaining wall is wrapped around the whole mold. Make sure the rubber is tight to the mold and duct tape is used to keep it in place.

Step 29

Mix up another batch of urethane and pour it over your sculpture.

Step 30

To keep the urethane positive from sticking to the urethane negative a separator is applied prior to pouring the negative. Each manufacturer of urethane will have suggested products you can use. Fill the mold about one inch over the highest point on the sculpture.

Step 31

Once the urethane is cured the rubber retaining wall can be removed. Even though the positive was made of urethane the negative could have been made of Ultracal-30. Clean up any rough edges with a rasp or knife.

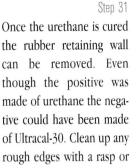

Step 32

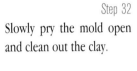

Slowly pry the mold open and clean out the clay.

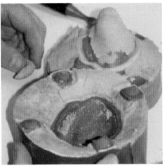

Step 33

In a microwave safe bowl pour in the desired amount of glycerin.

Step 34

In the same bowl add in your desired amount of Sorbitol.

Step 35

In a separate container, weigh out the desired amount of 300 blum gelatin.

Step 36
Heat up the glycerin and Sorbitol mixture in a microwave.

Step 37
Slowly stir in the gelatin into the heated glycerin and Sorbitol. Mix until smooth. Let the mixture completely cool after it is mixed.

Step 38
The gelatin mixture needs to be heated and cooled a few times to ensure all the gelatin crystals are completely melted and mixed in.

Step 39
As you wait for the gelatin to cool again mix up the flocking color, which will be added to the gelatin for color. Scoop small amounts of each color of the rayon flocking into a small bag.

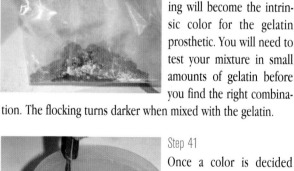

Step 40
Shake the contents of the bag to mix. The rayon flocking will become the intrinsic color for the gelatin prosthetic. You will need to test your mixture in small amounts of gelatin before you find the right combination. The flocking turns darker when mixed with the gelatin.

Step 41
Once a color is decided upon mix the flocking into the larger container of gelatin. Flocking is only one way to color gelatin. Almost any brand of liquid make-up can be used to tint the gelatin. Choose a liquid make-up that matches your performer and mix in with the gelatin in small amounts till the right color is achieved. When used with the flocking the color of the appliances can be very close to the performer's skin tone.

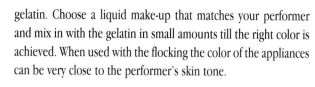

Step 42
Once the gelatin is colored it is now ready to be poured into the molds. Spray the surface of both halves of the molds with Epoxy Parafilm. Epoxy Parafilm is a standard mold release that works well to release the gelatin from most surfaces.

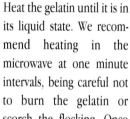

Step 43
Heat the gelatin until it is in its liquid state. We recommend heating in the microwave at one minute intervals, being careful not to burn the gelatin or scorch the flocking. Once completely liquid, pour into your mold.

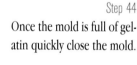

Step 44
Once the mold is full of gelatin quickly close the mold.

Step 45
Clamp the mold shut immediately after closing. This will ensure the thinnest edges possible.

Step 46
The Ultracal-30 mold is done in the same way. However, the gelatin can also be injected into the molds. Drill injection holes into the positive side of the mold, as shown in chapter 5,

then pour the heated gelatin into the injector gun and inject the gelatin into the closed mold.

the appliance, which means beautiful blending edges, but also indicates we should be extra careful that we do not damage that fragile edge.

Step 47

Another way to clamp the molds closed is with a mold strap. The strap is just as effective as the clamps and takes up a little less room in the lab. The clamp is faster to put on the mold.

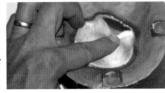

Step 53

Since there is no flashing to help lift an edge, try pushing down on a thick area of the appliance, enabling the edge to pull away from the mold; carefully apply powder to that edge. Continue to slowly work the appliance out of the mold in this fashion.

Step 48

Allow the gelatin to cool and set up for about 30 minutes.

Step 54

The removed prosthetic appliance, ready to apply.

Step 49

Once the gelatin is set, gently pry the two mold halves apart. Use slow gentle pressure. If you try to force the molds apart you may tear the appliance.

Step 50

Usually the positive will come out clean. If the gelatin is sticking to both molds try to free the positive first.

Step 51

Powder the exposed side of the gelatin appliance before trying to remove it from the second mold half. Un-powdered gelatin will stick to itself.

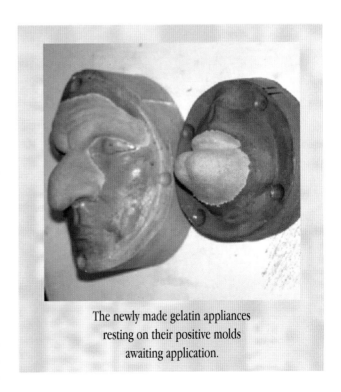

The newly made gelatin appliances resting on their positive molds awaiting application.

Step 52

Try to remove the appliance with the flashing. In this case the mold was closed so tightly that the flashing was cut away from

Gelatin Prosthetics   Chapter 6

Gelatin Prosthetic Application

Gelatin prosthetic appliances have grown in popularity in recent years, and now, with foam gelatin pieces being made, it seems gelatin will be around for awhile. Both types of pieces are applied in exactly the same way.

A station set-up for a gelatin prosthetic make-up. (Note the prosthetics in the lower left hand corner of the picture.) Before you ever get close to applying the prosthetics you need to seal them. The excess gelatin around a prosthetic is called the flashing. You should keep the flashing attached to the prosthetic until you have the piece glued to the skin. To prevent the flashing from accidentally tearing away from the piece, trim away all but 1/8 of an inch of it.

Step 1

Turn the prosthetic face down and clean away any mold release with 99% alcohol. Gently brush the front and back of the appliance. This will help the prosthetic appliance to stick to the glue. Now apply Pros-aide to the back of the piece. Do not apply Pros-aide to the edge or the flashing. Allow the adhesive to dry completely, then apply Kryolan Fixer Spray over the Pros-aide and allow that to dry. Repeat this step. The prosthetic is now ready to apply.

Step 2

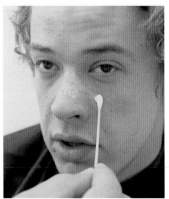

Apply Pros-aide to the skin in the area the prosthetic is to be applied. Allow the adhesive to dry completely.

Step 3

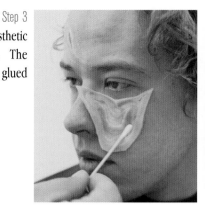

Then press the prosthetic into the adhesive. The edges should not be glued down yet.

Step 4

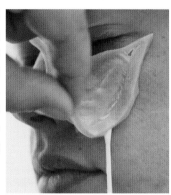

Lift the edge by the flashing and apply the adhesive under it, working all the way around the piece. Firmly press the edge into the dried adhesive. Be careful not to glue the flashing down.

Step 5

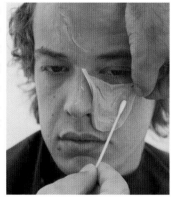

Using a cotton swab, dissolve the edge between the prosthetic and the flashing with witch hazel. Warm water will work, but it will cause the edges to become brittle.

Step 6

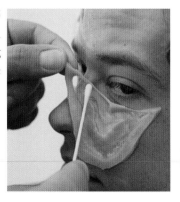

Use a rolling motion with the cotton swab, pushing the flashing away from the prosthetic.

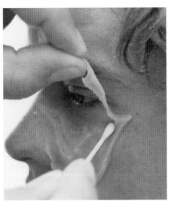

Step 7

Do not use too much witch hazel, a little goes a long way. (99% alcohol can be used to straighten out any folded edges.)

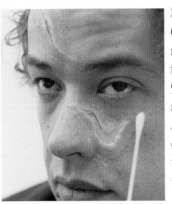

Step 8

Once the flashing is removed and the edge feathered into the skin, use 99% alcohol to straighten and lift any folded edges. Apply Pros-aide over the edge with the cotton swab to further blend the prosthetic into the skin.

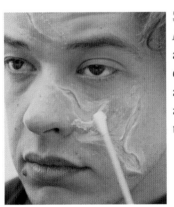

Step 9

After the prosthetic appliances are completely blended, use a rolling motion to apply a thin coat of Pros-aide over the entire prosthetic to seal it.

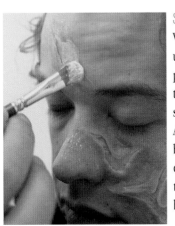

Step 10

With a filbert brush, pick up a generous amount of powder and press it into the edge. This will help subtle edges blend away. At this point you should be able to tell if your edges are blending or if they need to be further blended with Bondo.

Step 11

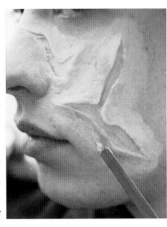

If you find you have a slight edge you can easily cover it with a small amount of Bondo. (A very thin mixture of Bondo is recommended, only doing the areas needed.) Texture can be added two ways. Rolling a wet cotton swab after the wet bondo or rolling another layer of Pros-aide over the driad Bondo.

Step 12

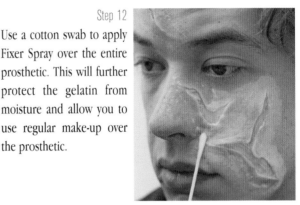

Use a cotton swab to apply Fixer Spray over the entire prosthetic. This will further protect the gelatin from moisture and allow you to use regular make-up over the prosthetic.

Step 13

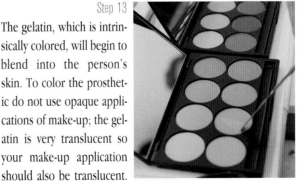

The gelatin, which is intrinsically colored, will begin to blend into the person's skin. To color the prosthetic do not use opaque applications of make-up; the gelatin is very translucent so your make-up application should also be translucent. Skin Illustrator and Reel Creations' tattoo inks are excellent choices to create a realistic texture and color to the prosthetic. The flocking added to the gelatin gives us a good base to start from, but additional color should be applied to the piece to create the subtle nuances in the skin, using Mud's cream make-up pallets.

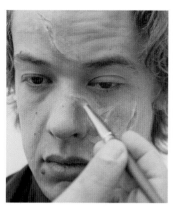

Step 14

Mix your base color with a small amount of 99% alcohol, and lightly stipple it over the appliances. Use three or four colors to create a realistic skin texture.

Step 18

Add Lake as a shadow in various areas. (Purple can also be used to make certain areas more "sore looking".)

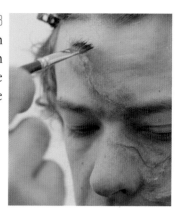

Step 15

Other colors such as red, green, and yellow, also need to be stippled into the appliances to help create reality.

Step 19

Line the opening of the cuts with black. If you completely paint the cut in it will look really deep. On the other hand, if you just line the inside of the cut it will look more superficial.

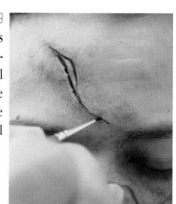

Step 16

Apply powder over the base colors to set them and to prevent them from mixing with the bruising colors. (Lake and #79 mixed together make a wonderful bruising color.)

Step 20

Mix regular blood with thick blood to create a fresh meaty look inside each of the cuts.

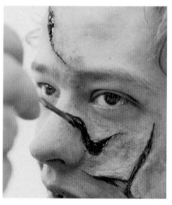

Step 17

Apply the red color over the openings of the cuts, then allow yourself to be creative and take the bruising out onto the skin.

Step 21

Add a small amount of regular blood to get the blood to run slightly.

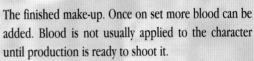

The finished make-up. Once on set more blood can be added. Blood is not usually applied to the character until production is ready to shoot it.

Notes:

Chapter 7

Polyurethane Foam Prostehetics

Polyurethane Prosthetic Construction

Prosthetic appliances serve many mediums including theater and theme park applications. Typically, these types of productions have limited budgets, so making prosthetics that can be re-used is a great way to cut costs, and the large number of appliances that may be used. There are a wide variety of urethane foams available to you and we will try to discuss as many as possible. There are two types of foam, rigid urethane and flexible urethane, and which one you choose will depend on your particular needs. Also, in those two categories you will find a wide variety of softness to hardness. Rigid urethanes are generally used for hard objects such as horns or some sort of bone effect, whereas, the flexible urethane foam can be used for noses and chins. Realize that the softest urethane foam is not nearly as soft as foam latex and will not move as well either, but it is much more durable and can be re-applied many times.

This is one example of urethane foam, sometimes called cold foam because no baking is required. A wide variety of urethane foams can be found at Burman Industries or Davis Dental Supply.

Step 1

We are using a plate mold of four noses and the mold is made of TC-1630, a rigid casting urethane. We are painting a mold release over both halves of the mold. A good mold release, capable of releasing a wide variety of flexible urethane foams, is Polysoft Mold Release.

Step 2

Every foam product has its own mixing ratios. Follow the manufactures instructions. A triple beam gram scale, or an accurate digital gram scale, work best to ensure proper proportions.

Step 3

After weighing out the required amounts of A and B components, mix the two together. A tongue depressor and a quick hand can be very effective to thoroughly mix the material, however we recommend a Jiffy Mixer to do the job without much effort. Mix the two for about 15 to 30 seconds, or until completely mixed. We also found the warmer the two components are the better they would foam. This type of foam must be used in a well ventilated area and with proper protection, such as, a respirator and rubber gloves.

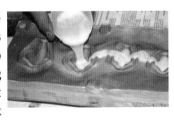

Step 4

As soon as the components are mixed, pour them into the mold. The foaming process happens almost immediately, so work quickly.

Step 5

Close the mold by placing the positive onto the negative, then strap or clamp the mold closed as the foam will continue to rise and lift the positive mold right off the negative.

Step 6

Allow the foam to completely cure before opening the mold. If the mold is opened too soon the foam may collapse or may stick inside one or both of the halves.

Step 7

To test if the foam is ready to be pulled from the mold, peel up a small section of flashing and squeeze it; if it remains collapsed it needs more time to cure, and if it bounces back then it is ready to pull.

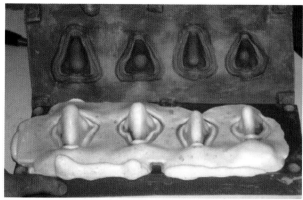
Step 8

Slowly pry the molds apart in the same fashion you would de-mold any other prosthetic material. The finished prosthetics are now ready to be applied.

Application

A urethane prosthetic is applied in the same fashion as a foam latex prosthetic appliance. Its durability allows this type of prosthetic to be removed and re-applied several times.

Notes:

Chapter 8

Silicone Prosthetics

Silicone GFA Construction

This type of prosthetic is applied virtually the same way as a gelatin prosthetic. The main difference is you cannot dissolve the edge with witch hazel. We did a test with both silicone and gelatin, making appliances of each type by running the different materials in the same molds. We then applied each to the same performer, getting exactly the same results. The big difference was the silicone GFA moved and felt real.

Step 1

Life casting and the positive mold construction start out the same way as all the other types of prosthetics. The sculpture is where things change a bit. Instead of doing multiple pieces, such as a large foam latex prosthetic make-up, you can make the prosthetic in one big piece. Foam latex shrinks 15% whereas baked silicone does not, so silicone can be used without breaking it down. This can save a great deal of time during pre-production.

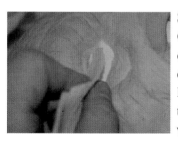

Step 2

Other than not breaking down, the sculpture is basically done the same way. Prior to starting this sculpture we coated the positive with a couple of coats of Alcoat, enabling us to later lift the sculpture off the positive.

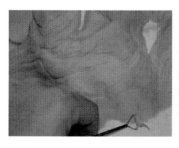

Step 3

Some artists suggest ending the blending edge a little sooner than you would normally. We didn't find this helped that much.

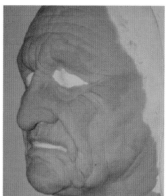

Step 4

You could simply mold the sculpture at this point, however we chose to break this sculpture down the same way a break-down sculpture for a foam latex make-up would be done.

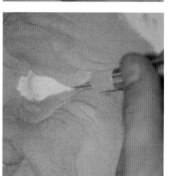

Step 5

Using an X-acto knife carefully cut the clay into the desired sections.

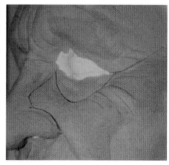

Step 6

Each section is planned from the beginning. The sculpture is kept thin where the cuts are anticipated. Complete all the cuts at one time.

Step 7

Set the sculpture into a container of water and allow to soak. The Alcoat that was painted all over the positive, prior to starting the sculpture, will dissolve in the water, allowing the sculpture to be lifted off the positive without much damage.

Step 8

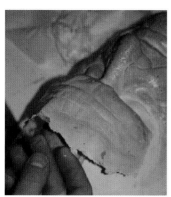

Once the sculpture starts to move a little you can use a thin piece of plastic to help lift the fragile sculpture off the positive.

Step 9

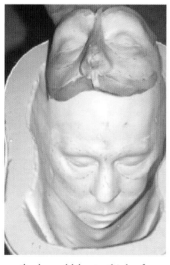

All the pieces are lifted off the cast and laid aside. A vacuform copy of the original lifecast is generally used to cradle the prosthetics while the new positives are made.

Step 10

A silicone copy is made of the positive mold, then the various areas that will support the prosthetics. In this instance this mold will be used for the eye bags. The mold is made of a dental stone, but you could use Ultracal-30 or even a urethane molding material. Also, this is the simple way to break down a sculpture and mold; the better method would be to think of your sculpture as the prosthetic appliance. You lift off the first clay section, that section becoming the last prosthetic to be put on when doing the make-up. Now, blend the surrounding clay pieces into the cast and then cast that area in silicone or alginate, so when you make a positive mold from that negative mold you will be able to re-apply the removed sculpture to the new mold, but the new mold will have the edges of the other prosthetics and you will be able to blend this sculpture into those.

Step 11

The new positive molds are made the same as in chapter 6 and are now ready to receive the sculptures.

Step 12

The neck and forehead positives are the only molds not made into cylinder molds because of their size and shape.

Step 13

All of the sculptures are placed on the positive molds; each sculpture will need to be blended onto the positive and repaired of any damage incurred during the transfer process. Once all the sculptures are repaired a final texture is pressed into them to unify all the sculptures into one skin texture.

Step 14

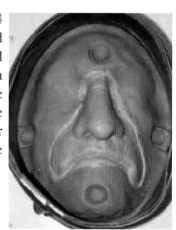

A clay wall is laid around the sculpture and around the keys, leaving only an eighth of an inch of positive mold showing around the sculpture. Also, a rubber dam is wrapped around the positive mold.

Step 15

All the cylinder molds are prepared this same way.

Step 16

The cylinder molds were all filled with TC-1630, a rigid casting urethane. Ultracal-30 or the same dental stone used for the positive molds, could have been used to make the negative molds of our cylinder molds.

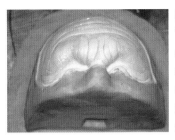

Step 17

The forehead required the same clay wall around the sculpture; however, instead of wrapping the mold in a rubber dam we created a clay pad around the mold.

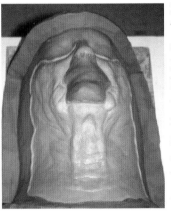

Step 18

The neck was again the same technique as the forehead. These molds are then brushed up over the sculptures, creating a negative mold that is about 3/4 of an inch thick, following the contours of the sculpture. This is a more traditional molding technique.

Step 19

All of the molds for this multi-piece prosthetic make-up.

Step 20

Drill small extrusion holes all around the edge for the silicone gel to escape as you are injecting through a larger center hole.

Step 21

Foam latex mold release is used as the separator for silicone gel filled prosthetics. Each manufacturer will have its own recommendations for the type of separator to use.

Step 22

The encapsulator is the material that will form the skin of the appliance, allowing the silicone to be glued to skin and made easier to color.

Step 23

Spray two layers of the encapsulator over all the positives. Go beyond the blending edge to ensure the skin on the positive attaches to the skin on the negative.

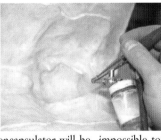

Step 24

Also spray two layers of the encapsulator over the inside of the negative mold. Make sure you spray an even coat, otherwise, when the piece is de-molded the areas not covered with the encapsulator will be impossible to color.

Step 25

Now carefully close each mold. The encapsulator sticks to itself and if you close the molds improperly the skin may stick together in an undisirable area, causing you to possibly have to re-do the skin.

Step 26

The silicone gel is poured into a large or wide mouth container. In this container color or flocking can be added to tint the gel the shade you want.

Step 27

Weigh out small amounts of the gel and add catalyst to it, depending on the manufacturer's requirements.

Step 28

Use a large syringe capable of holding enough material to fill one mold and draw the material into it.

Step 29

Inject the silicone gel into the closed molds until all the extrusion holes leak silicone. Make sure all the molds are tightly strapped or clamped.

Step 30

Leave the syringe in the injector hole to keep positive pressure inside the mold. After the gel is cured the syringe is easily removed.

Step 31

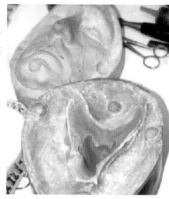

This particular system does not require baking; just let it cure then de-mold. Slowly open the molds, being careful not to tear the prosthetics.

Step 32

The finished prosthetic is an intrinsically colored appliance, with an outer skin that moves independently of the inner skin, which is attached to the face. This results in a very realistic movement.

Step 33

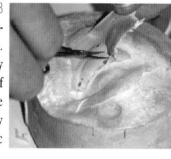

Carefully peel the prosthetics from the positive molds. (Usually the piece will stay with the positive because of the extrusion points. Those points need to be cut away as you peel the prosthetic off.)

Step 34

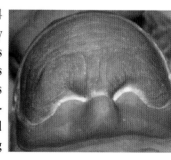

You should not have any large areas of flashing as you see here. This means that the skin that was sprayed on both the positive and the negative did not stick to itself, allowing the gel to escape.

Step 35

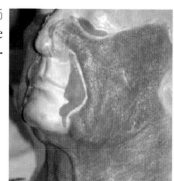

The same happened here but not as bad. This particular piece was still usable.

Silicone GFA Application

A step-by-step look at the entire process of how a multiple piece prosthetic make-up should be applied using silicone gel-filled appliances.

The model for the multi-piece silicone gel filled appliances.

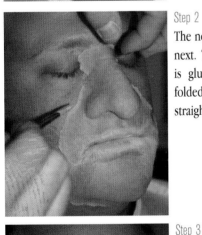

Step 1

The chin is the first piece to go on, using Pros-aide adhesive to glue it down and the same techniques we employ for other prosthetics.

Step 2

The nose and upper lip are next. The entire prosthetic is glued down, with any folded or wrinkled edges straightened with alcohol.

Step 3

The neck and cheek pieces are the most tricky. Apply under the chin first by applying a layer of adhesive to the skin, then to the appliance. Allow both to dry, then press them together. Next, work up each cheek, gluing as you go. Finally, glue down the

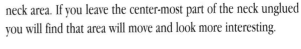

neck area. If you leave the center-most part of the neck unglued you will find that area will move and look more interesting.

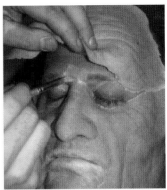

Step 4

The forehead piece is anchored between the brows.

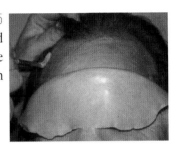

Step 5

Fold the prosthetic forward and apply adhesive to the rest of the forehead, then unfold the piece.

Step 6

The eye bags are applied last. Once all the pieces are attached you can begin the blending process.

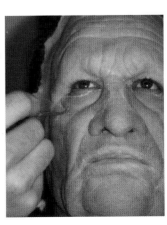

Step 7

Pros-aide is used over all the edges to help blend them. If an edge is a little thick a small amount of bondo can be used to help fill those gaps.

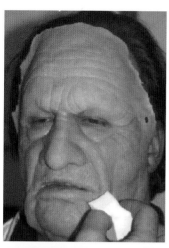

Step 8

The excess powder is removed with alcohol or a damp sponge. The prosthetics will take on a very translucent fleshy look.

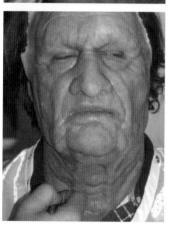

Step 9

Washes of color are stippled over the face to create that modeling effect real skin has. Five or six colors will be mixed with 99% alcohol and stippled so an irregular pattern is achieved.

Step 10

Apply the colors unevenly and allow some areas to stay light.

Step 11

Red, yellow, and green colors can be stippled into prosthetic. These colors really start to add that surface color. Do not use too much, the yellow and green can be mixed with base colors to tone them down. It is suggested the

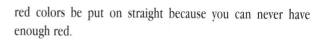

red colors be put on straight because you can never have enough red.

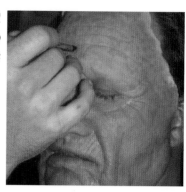

Step 12

Age spots are added to the forehead to give surface texture.

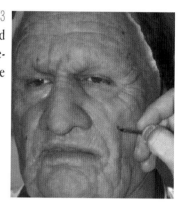

Step 13

Veins, capillaries, and moles are added to create translucency in the make-up.

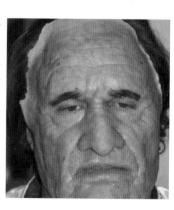

Step 14

Lace eyebrows are added. The lace was applied with a silicone adhesive, being careful not to mess up the make-up as it was applied. The lips were given a touch of color.

Step 15

A wig is applied over the actor's head and the top edge of the prosthetic forehead.

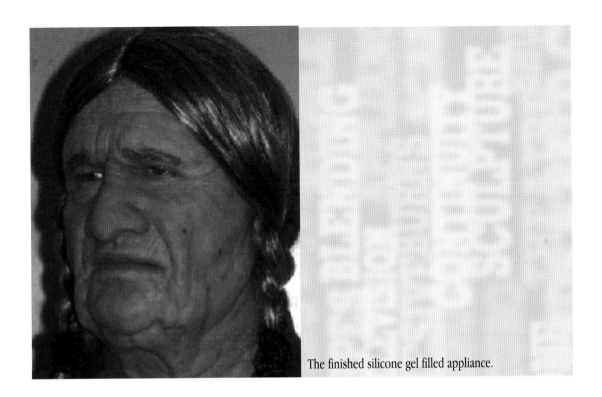

The finished silicone gel filled appliance.

Notes:

Chapter 9

Airbrush

Airbrushing Basics

Most airbrushes are designed to allow any water-based paints, oils, adhesives, enamels, acrylics, and make-ups to flow through them. Any free-flowing material with the consistency of milk could be sprayed through an airbrush.

First we will talk about the variety of tools available to you, and we will de-mystify the tool altogether. Many people believe the airbrush is a magic tool, the end-all tool to any art project. The airbrush is indeed a great tool, but it is just that, another tool we utilize, as make-up artists, to create different effects. Just as we use a sponge or a brush, one is not better than the other, they are just different from each other.

The two airbrushes we will be discussing will be the Paasche H and VL airbrushes. One is a single-action airbrush and the other is a double-action airbrush. Even though we will be only discussing these two airbrushes, most of the information will apply to other single and double action airbrushes.

Paasche airbrushes are made with 3 different size nozzles designed to accommodate various fluids and spray patterns; the 1,3,and 5. The nozzle size should be selected according to the viscosity of the fluid. Thicker fluids require a larger nozzle and more pressure.

Pattern size is determined by the size of the nozzle, for the double-action airbrush, and the tip, needle, and color adjusting parts for the single-action airbrushes, as well as the distance from the painting surface.

The Paasche model H is a single action airbrush. This airbrush is very durable and will allow almost anything to be sprayed through it. In extreme cases, we have sprayed rubber cement and silicone caulking through it; it is very easy to clean and maintain and simple to operate.

The Paasche model VL is a double action airbrush. This airbrush is the workhorse of the industry and is used by a large number of artists. It's uses range from the painting of animatronic skins to the application of body make-up. This airbrush is somewhat more difficult to use because it requires a little more hand and eye coordination. This airbrush may clog more often and require additional cleaning when spraying thicker fluids or adhesives.

Keep your airbrush clean and in good working order. Follow the instructions that come with the airbrush and it will be a vital tool in your make-up kit.

Air Supply

There are a wide variety of ways to provide air to your airbrush, the most common being a compressor. There are many different types of compressors to choose from. The challenge is, finding the right one for you. It is important to understand how a compressor works before you decide which one is best for you. An air compressor does just what it's name implies. A compressor uses a diaphragm or a piston to draw air into a chamber, then it pushes the air out at the same rate. Here are a few of your choices: One is just a compressor motor, which is usually very inexpensive, but does not supply an even airflow and is very noisy. The next choice is a compressor with a tank attached. The benefit of this type is an even airflow and a motor that shuts off once the tank is full, only turning on to refill the tank. However, this type of compressor is still very noisy when the motor is on. Your third choice is a silent compressor, which has a motor and a tank. This motor is insulated and runs much quieter than its predecessors, but this kind of compressor is expensive, usually three or four times the cost of a standard compressor. There are other alternatives available. Carbon dioxide gas can also be used as an air supply, even though carbon dioxide isn't, technically, air. Art stores carry carbon dioxide in spray paint size cans, however they regularly freeze up and run out quickly. You can keep the small cans of carbon dioxide from freezing by submerging them in about an inch of warm water. (You can purchase carbon dioxide canisters from a welding supply, that will last much longer and are re-fillable.) Canisters come in various sizes, 10-lb., 20-lb., with some suppliers stocking even larger sizes; 10-lb. tanks will typically last about ten hours of moderate spraying and a 20-lb. tank about 20 hours.

Maintenance

Before laying your airbrush aside, even for a short period of time, empty it of all color; then run water, or the proper solvent for the medium you are using, trough it to clean all residue left behind. There will be times when paint will dry inside the airbrush and begin to clog it, greatly affecting its performance if it is not cleaned. To thoroughly clean the airbrush you will have to dismantle it. Refer to the diagrams of each airbrush, (usually provided in the instruction booklet that comes with a new airbrush) to ensure proper disassembly and assembly. With the airbrush completely taken apart you will be able to thoroughly clean every portion of it.

Operating the Airbrush

There are three movements that the beginner needs to become familiar with. First, hold the airbrush so the tip of the forefinger rests on the button that activates the airflow. Press down on the button to start air flowing through the brush. Secondly, for the H airbrush, spin the color adjusting part with your other hand to increase and decrease the flow of paint. For the VL airbrush, pulling back on the button will start the flow of paint. Thirdly, move your hand to the right and left, and up and down.

The distance the tip of the airbrush is from the work surface will vary the size of your spray pattern. The farther you are away, the wider the spray pattern; the closer you are to the surface, the thinner the line. Build up your colors gradually– too much paint or a surface that is overly wet will start to run.

Airbrush Exercises

Here are some simple exercises we recommend to begin mastering the control of the airbrush. The following lessons are designed to be done on paper, and should be done in the fashion described. These lessons should also be carried on to the types of surfaces you will be airbrushing, such as skin, foam, or silicone.

Exersise #1

This exercise is designed to give you some basic control over the airbrush. We will use the process of making dots the activity to gain that control. Start out on paper before moving to skin and use a water-based make-up for easy clean up. To familiarize yourself with the feel and the functions of the airbrush, practice spraying air from the tool. Now, hold the airbrush about one inch from the paper, begin spraying air, and then slowly pull back on the trigger to introduce make-up. Practice this process until you are able to place dots accurately, without spraying too much make-up

onto the paper. If you pull back on the trigger too far, make-up will pool in one spot, creating a puddle. Next, adjust the size of the dots and the intensity of the dots. To accomplish this you will have to allow more make-up to spray out of the airbrush and you will have to increase the distance between the airbrush and the surface you are painting. Once you have mastered this skill you will be able to place color anywhere you need and in any quantity..

Exersise #2

This exercise will enable you to evenly apply make-up with the airbrush, as well as blend color from one area to another. When using an airbrush for make-up application, many times we are applying base or trying to make a body all one color. Again, start out on paper before trying this on skin. White paper will show you the areas where you need more coverage. Practice moving the airbrush left and right over the paper. Make sure you start to move your hand right to left before releasing any color. Otherwise, where you begin and end your move will be heavier than in the middle, creating spots at the beginning and end of your move. Another technique, used to achieve the same result, is working in circular motion with the airbrush to create smooth, even coverage over a large area. The final result should be a thin, even application of color without any puddles.

Exersise #3

Creating darts with the airbrush is the process of graduating a line from narrow to broad. Practice by moving the airbrush then releasing more color as you move along a straight lines and at the same time move the airbrush away from the surface. You will create the effect of a fine line that gets wider at one end. The airbrush should always be moving when you stop spraying or you will end up with a dot at the end of the line. Repeat this exercise until you feel comfortable making darts.

Exersise #4

Spray dots in a grid pattern in the same fashion you made the dots in the first exercise. Next, connect the dots with thin straight lines of color that are the same consistency from dot to dot. Continue till you can comfortably create any line without over spraying or pooling at the ends of the lines. Again, create another grid of dots and connect each dot with a curved line. (Make sure each line is uniform in consistence and thickness).

Exersise #5

The final exercise is to help you apply color in layers. Start by spraying a thin application of color in a horizontal line about two inches in height. Next, spray another horizontal line with the same thickness of color about one inch in height, but this time overlap the previous line, covering the bottom half of the first line. Finally, do a third line, again the same thickness of color, but only half an inch thick. The result should be a nice gradation of color from light on top to dark on the bottom.

Continue to practice the exercises described as often as possible. The more you are able to practice these techniques the faster you will master using the airbrush. The airbrush can be an extremely versatile tool and a valuable addition to your make-up case. Feel free to experiment and employ the various techniques we have discussed.

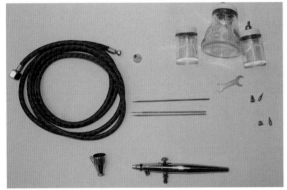

A complete Paasche VL airbrush set. These are all the parts that come in the set.

The color cups and bottles that come with the Paasche VL set. You have a variety of choices due to the many different applications you may be doing. The small color cup is designed for minimal amounts of color usually associated with detail work. The bigger glass bottles are for larger amounts of color and bigger areas such as body painting.

Learning the Tool

The following is a photo breakdown of how to dismantle the airbrush and its inner workings. We show how to take apart just one available airbrush. It is the airbrush that we use in our class. Do realize that not every airbrush will come apart in this fashion, but once you understand how this double action airbrush is put together, and comprehend its inner workings, you will find that

other double action airbrushes are very similar and just as easy to figure out. This is the best way to become one with the tool. The more comfortable you are taking the tool apart the more at ease you will become with the tool itself.

Disassembling the Airbrush

Use this step-by-step photo breakdown to guide you through the process of disassembling the airbrush. Each photograph represents a part that is removed from the airbrush and we suggest that the parts be laid out in order so you will know how the parts go back on.

Step 1

The VL Airbrush is a double action syphon feed airbrush. It is not the most expensive airbrush you can purchase, but it is one of the most durable and reliable ones on the market. This is what the assembled airbrush should look like.

Step 2

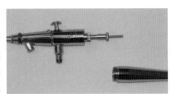

Remove the handle by unscrewing it and then set aside. Some artists will use the airbrush as you see here; this allows the artist the ability to quickly clear a clog or adjust the needle while working.

Step 3

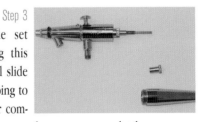

Unscrew the needle set screw. By loosening this screw the needle will slide out, but if you are going to clean the airbrush or completely take it apart, remove the set screw completely.

Step 4

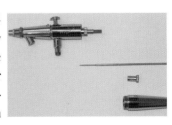

Pull out the needle. Be very careful with this needle. The point is very easy to bend or crush. It comes in three different sizes and must match the aircap and the tip.

Step 5

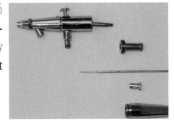

Unscrew the rocker assembly set screw. Completely remove the screw and set aside.

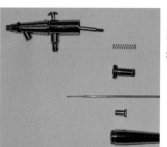

Step 6

Pull out the compression spring. Set aside.

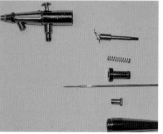

Step 7

Carefully slide out the rocker assembly. Since the needle passes through the inside of this assembly it may be necessary to clean with a pipe cleaner.

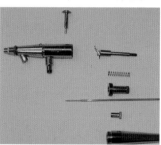

Step 8

Pull the trigger up out of the top of the airbrush.

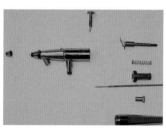

Step 9

Unscrew the aircap from the front of the airbrush. This aircap comes in three different sizes and must match the needle and the tip.

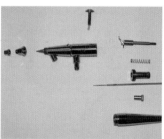

Step 10

Unscrew the aircap body from the front of the airbrush.

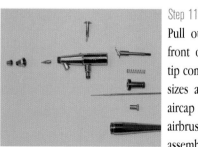

Step 11

Pull out the tip from the front of the airbrush. The tip comes in three different sizes and must match the aircap and the needle. The airbrush is completely disassembled. There are two other areas that can come apart, but the need to separate these areas would be an infrequent occurrence.

Changing the Spray Pattern

The next four pictures represent your choice in the spray pattern of the tool. Your three choices are listed in numerical value. Number one is the smallest pattern on this airbrush and the number five is the largest. When changing your airbrush to a new spray pattern the numbers on all the parts must match.

Here are the three aircaps in close-up; note how they are marked. The number one aircap is marked with a line. The number three and number five aircaps

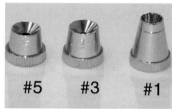

are marked with their respective numbers, which are stamped into the surface.

The tips are not marked with any identifying marks, but, visually, you can tell which is larger, the smallest one being the number one and the largest, num-

ber five. Again, these must be used with corresponding needles and aircaps.

The needles. The fourth needle is a reamer, used only to clean hardened paint from the inside of your airbrush. Visually, you can see the smallest tip is the number one needle and the largest tip is the number five needle. If you look closely at the bottoms of the three needles you will see marks there.

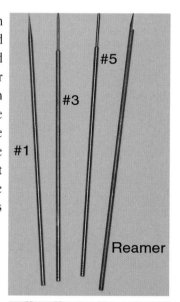

This is a close-up of the back side of the needles and their marks. One line going around the needle is the number one needle, three lines going around the needle is the number three needle,

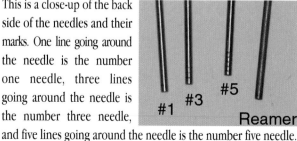

and five lines going around the needle is the number five needle.

Assembling the Airbrush

Again we have used photographs to illustrate how the airbrush is re-assembled. However, you should be able to assemble it easily by reversing the order in which you took it apart.

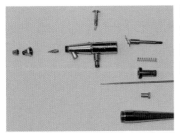

Step 1

To reassemble the airbrush hold the main body in your hand.

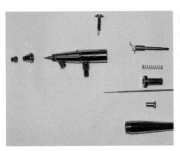

Step 2

Push the tip into the hole on the front of the airbrush. Select a size tip for the type of work you will be doing.

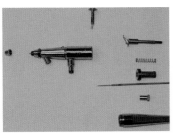

Step 3

Screw on the aircap. Tighten it only finger tight so that it can be removed easily while working, or for quick changes of the needles and tips.

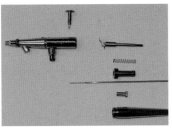

Step 4

Screw on the aircap, again only finger tight. The aircap has to be the same size as the tip. These front pieces must go on first to ensure that they are not damaged or likely to do harm to the needle.

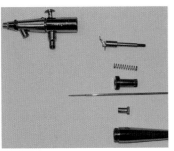

Step 5

Push the trigger down into the airbrush. The trigger has an opening in the middle of the brush that needs to be positioned, so the needle can pass straight through it. Also, the bottom of the trigger needs to slip into the round opening at the base of the airbrush. When the trigger is installed properly the trigger has a spongy feel. Be careful turning the airbrush over at this stage, as the only thing holding the trigger in is the needle.

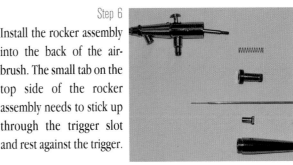

Step 6

Install the rocker assembly into the back of the airbrush. The small tab on the top side of the rocker assembly needs to stick up through the trigger slot and rest against the trigger.

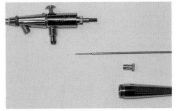

Step 7

Slip the compression spring over the rocker assembly.

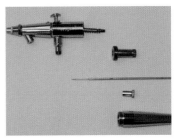

Step 8

Screw in the rocker assembly set screw. Tighten all the way.

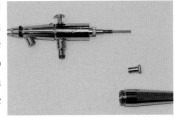

Step 9

Push the needle through the rocker assembly, the trigger, and snuggly into the tip. Do not jam it in as you may damage the needle or the tip.

Step 10

Screw on the needle set screw. Lightly tighten with your fingers.

The completely reassembled VL Airbrush, ready for use.

Airbrush Make-up

It is important to understand the airbrush is a tool to apply make-up with, not a make-up technique. The airbrush can be used to create interesting effects, as well as speed up a make-up application. The following make-up is an exercise in highlight and shadow and can be achieved with any other make-up tool of your choice. Here we used the airbrush to illustrate the speed and ease in which you may apply make-up.

The model, draped with a cover cloth, is ready for the make-up application.

Step 1

The first color sprayed is a brown make-up used to do the initial shading and to sketch out the design on our character.

Step 2

Shading is applied under the cheekbone and to the temple area. We will continue to apply shadow to all the depressions in the one side of her face and neck. Slowly darken the shadows to the depth that you need. The airbrush works very well to model these shadows with the one color, making some areas darker and other areas lighter with the same color.

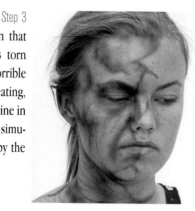

Step 3

To create the illusion that part of her face was torn off, to reveal the horrible monster we are creating, we are adding a dark line in a jagged formation to simulate the shadow cast by the edge of skin.

Step 4

Lines are added to the skin for texture by holding the airbrush closer to the skin and moving your hand quickly across the area. These darker lines should fade at both ends of the line. You can use this technique to create wrinkles around the eyes.

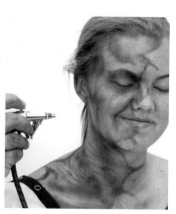

Step 5

Introduce green make-up into the shadows to deepen them and to add color. Move the airbrush closer and then further away as you spray in quick bursts. This will achieve a modeled effect. Green should be sprayed lightly over the face to give it a greenish tint.

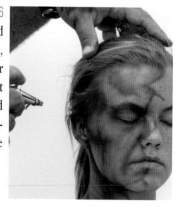

Step 6

Yellow make-up is sprayed onto the highlights. Again, because of the nature of our character, we are applying it unevenly. Hit all the raised areas first then use the yellow to highlight some of the wrinkles.

Step 7

We are using black make-up in the airbrush to deepen all the shadows. It is being sprayed along the torn off edge as well as in the deepest areas of the facial shadows.

Step 8

Now, we will use more traditional tools like a make-up brush to add black cream make-up along the very edge of the torn skin. The airbrush creates a soft color and works perfectly to shade an area, however we need that black color to have a sharp edge and more intensity. Using a make-up brush does this perfectly.

Step 9

Using different brushes and different colors to complete the small details like dark brown to sharpen the wrinkles and black to line the eye. You can use teal for veins and red for small capillaries.

Step 10

We used a larger brush with a deeper red to stipple redness around the eye, to create a little warmth and soreness. We did the same thing at the corner of the mouth and side of the nose, and we used it to transition some of the highlights with a few of the shadows.

Step 11

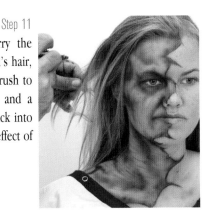

We decided to carry the look into our model's hair, so we used the airbrush to spray a little white and a small amount of black into it. This created the effect of dull unhealthy hair.

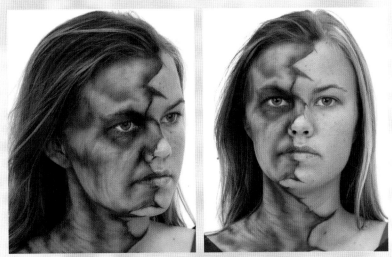

The finished make-up.

Airbrush Prosthetics

The prosthetic portion of this make-up is done exactly like it was explained in previous chapters. However, the difference is in how we apply the make-up. It is possible to use the airbrush to do the bulk of the make-up or to use the airbrush to create the subtle nuances you are trying to achieve. (Prosthetics have the added problem of requiring you to use certain types of make-up.) Depending on whom you ask you will get a plethora of options as to which type of make-up or paint you can use, but in the end it is what works best for you that is the best option.

The model prior to the application of the make-up.

Step 1

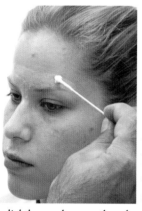

Test fitting the forehead prosthetic appliance on the model's forehead. Prior to using any glue it is important to see how the prosthetic appliance fits around the eyes and over the eyebrows. Once you know exactly where the appliance should sit then some artists like to lightly powder over the edges of the appliance. Once the prosthetic appliance is removed a residue of powder is left around area occupied by the appliance.

Step 2

Apply Pros-aide adhesive to the skin and to the inside of the prosthetic appliance, remember to work in small manageable areas, do not just apply adhesive over the entire area. . The adhesive can be used on the skin or the appliance only, however, for the best bond we recommend using it on both surfaces. Allow the adhesive to dry completely.

Step 3

Press the prosthetic appliance onto the skin, the adhesive acts as contact adhesive and will bond instantly upon contact. Pressing firmly as you carefully position the appliance.

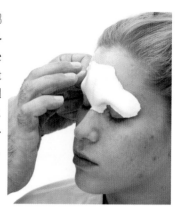

Step 4

Lift the edge of the prosthetic appliance and apply adhesive lightly behind it. Then carefully lay the delicate edge into the adhesive, pressing with your finger to lay it flat.

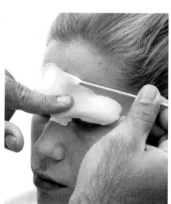

Step 5

With a brush and a small amount of alcohol work the edge straight and smooth. The alcohol will allow you to loosen the edge and straighten it without damaging it.

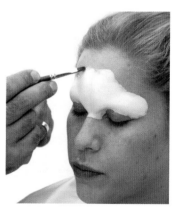

Step 6

Use a small amount of Pros-aide with a cotton swab, and apply the adhesive over the edge of the prosthetic appliance. Lightly stipple the adhesive on with the cotton swab to blend the edges into the skin. Slowly build up the layers until it is perfectly blended. You may need to use a small amount of bondo to fill in larger imperfections.

Step 7

Powder the edges thoroughly before moving on. Using a brush press the powder onto the edge, making sure every exposed bit of adhesive is well covered.

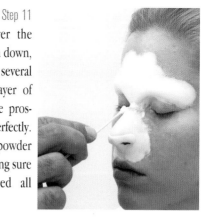

Step 11

Apply adhesive over the edges to blend them down, you may need to do several layers or even a layer of bondo to blend the prosthetic appliance perfectly. With a brush press powder into the edges, making sure you have powdered all exposed adhesive.

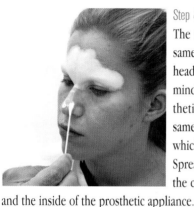

Step 8

The nose is applied in the same fashion as the forehead. One thing to keep in mind is to test fit both prosthetic appliances at the same time so you will know which one to apply first. Spread the adhesive over the center area of the nose and the inside of the prosthetic appliance.

Step 12

Application of the ear prosthetics is done exactly the same way as any other prosthetic appliance. Apply adhesive to the ear and to the inside of the prosthetic appliance.

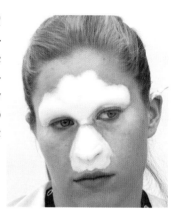

Step 9

Once the adhesive is dry, press the prosthetic appliance to the nose. Ensure the nostrils are lining up properly.

Step 13

Press the ear prosthetic over the actual ear. Be extra careful not to trap hair under the prosthetic appliance. 99% alcohol can be used to pull out any stray hairs or to straighten out any problem edge.

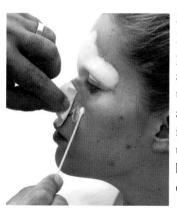

Step 10

Lift up on the edge of the prosthetic appliance and apply adhesive on the skin under the prosthetic appliance. Then press the edge into the adhesive. You can use 99% alcohol and a brush to lay the edge down.

Step 14

Apply adhesive behind the edges of the prosthetic appliance and press them down. Again you can blend the prosthetic appliance by using more adhesive to soften the edge.

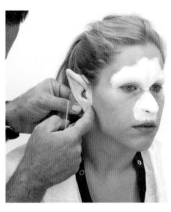

Step 15

Repeat this procedure for the other ear. Once all the prosthetic appliances are adhered and well blended, you should apply a layer of adhesive over all the appliances to seal them. This will keep the make-up from soaking into them irregularly.

Step 19

Base color is now applied to the prosthetics by mixing a few shades of the rubber mask grease paint together and then stippling them on over the red, carefully blending it into the surrounding skin.

Step 16

Powder the appliances thoroughly before proceeding. Use a powder puff to ensure all the adhesive has been powdered.

Step 20

The ears, because they are already tinted a skin tone, do not need the initial red color added. However, we still apply the same base color over them. You may need to apply two or three shades of base to get the right combination of skin color.

Step 17

Notice how much more yellow the facial appliances are than the ear appliances. The ear prosthetic appliances have been tinted a color in the mixing process of the foam latex. Whereas, the facial appliances are the natural foam color. To counteract that light yellow color of the appliances we use a brick colored rubber mask grease paint.

Step 21

Apply powder over all the rubber mask grease paint make-up to create a good base for the airbrush make-up. (We could have applied Pax Paint to the prosthetics and then airbrushed more Pax Paint on top of that.) We are going to use a liquid airbrush make-up so we chose to use well-powdered rubber mask grease paint as our color base.

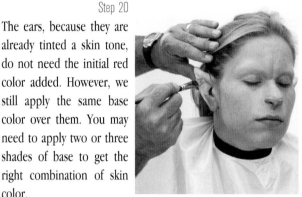

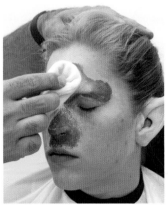

Step 18

Keep the brick color only on the prosthetic appliances. Powder the rubber mask grease paint completely before adding another color. Otherwise the red will mix with the base color and turn the base color a funny shade of pink.

Step 22

We are using a Paasche VL airbrush to apply our make-up. Any double action airbrush will work. Choose one that you are familiar with. Test the airflow on the model prior to adding any make-up into the color cup. This will help the model to become accustomed to the sensation of the air blast. We have set the compressor to put out about six pounds of pressure.

Step 23

White make-up is lightly sprayed down the center of the face. When working near the eyelids try to angle the airbrush down so you do not force make-up under the lids. Also, when spraying around the nose and mouth, we usually ask the model to take a breath and hold it until we have passed over that area.

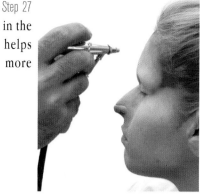

Step 27

Adding more color in the natural shadows helps the colors look more interesting.

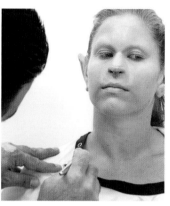

Step 24

We worked the white across most of the highlight areas and mostly through the center of the face and neck, spraying small amounts at a time to ensure an even application.

Step 28

We used the same color to shadow the sides of the nose and to deepen the eyes. What is nice about the airbrush is the ease of laying the colors on, and the way they overlap.

Step 25

We used water to clear the airbrush of any excess white and to clean it out. Then we mixed up a deep reddish purple color to spray along the hairline, spraying it lightly to create a soft effect.

Step 29

To create some texture we are adding a dark purple color in a tight spotted pattern over our red. You could use stencils at this point to create interesting textures.

Step 26

Using the same color we create a more intense look by moving a little closer with the airbrush and allowing a little more paint to flow. To achieve this simply pull back a little further on the trigger.

Step 30

The purple color is also used to deepen some of the shadows inside the ear and along the neck area.

Step 31

A vibrant red is sprayed over the top of the model's hair. We streak the color into her hair to mix with her natural color. We then sprayed black into the base of the hair for depth at the roots of the hair.

Step 33

A deep purple eye shadow is applied over the lids to define them and create drama.

Step 32

A soft pink cream make-up is applied to the nose to give it a nice fleshy look.

Step 34

The same soft pink color, but this time a lip make-up, is applied to the lips to finish off the make-up.

The finished prosthetic make-up.

Chapter 10

Bald Cap

Introduction to Bald Caps

A bald cap is used for a variety of reasons, the obvious one being to make an actor look bald, but it also can be used under prosthetic appliances as a base for them. When used under prosthetic appliances the cap is usually made of latex and generally does not have to be applied perfectly, because it will be completely covered by the prosthetic appliances. When the cap is applied for the purpose of making someone look bald, every care must be taken to apply it as flawlessly as possible.

The first step in using a bald cap is to decide which type of cap will be used and in which medium it will be seen. (i.e.: film, tv, or stage) There are three types of bald caps that could be utilized in order to create the effect of a bald head. The first is made of vulcanized rubber, the second, a vinyl plastic, and the third, foam latex.

The first two, rubber and vinyl, have an inherent problem in that the back of the head is missing the occipital bone. On a real bald head there are lots of dents and bumps, and at the base of the skull there is a bony protrusion called the occipital bone. A bald cap is glued on only at the edges because the hair is in the way, so wherever there is hair the cap is very smooth, which really limits the production's ability to shoot the back of the head. If the cap is for a variety show like "Saturday Night Live" or "MadTV", in which the cap is used for a small segment, then it doesn't matter if the occipital bone is present. However, if the cap is for a film, and the person needs to look believably bald, there are a couple of ways to do it. Apply a rubber or a vinyl cap, then apply a prosthetic to the back of the head to simulate the occipital bone, or use a Foam Latex cap that is specially made for that person, with all the details added since it is a sculpted prosthetic.

Many times a production will ask the performer to shave his or her head, particularly if the bald person has a major role in the film. If it's a small part, a bald cap will be used, but it is very important to explain to production the limits and the advantages of each type of cap, enabling them to make an informed decision about which cap to use. This includes asking the actor to shave his/her head, or being very careful of the way they shoot the cap. Proper communication will ensure everyone involved will know what to expect from the bald cap.

Rubber Bald Caps

A rubber cap can be made from almost any vulcanized latex available. We have found Pliatex Mold Rubber, which is used as a molding compound, to be the strongest while staying extremely thin. Pliatex Mold Rubber is available from Sculpture House in New York. This type of cap may be purchased pre-made or can be made fairly easily using a bald cap form. Most make-up suppliers either carry a rubber bald cap bearing their name or one made by an outside source. Another latex cap, available at most costume and Halloween type stores, is the Woochie Bald Cap. The other choice you have is to make your own cap from Pliatex Mold Rubber, using a bald cap form. Make-up Designory and Kryolan both offer a reasonably priced form. Because this cap is made of rubber it is important to remember only Rubber Mask Grease Paint (RMGP) can be used to color it.

Rubber Mask Grease Paint palette.

Vinyl Bald Caps

A vinyl cap, sometimes referred to as a plastic cap, is made of a vinyl acetate mixture dissolved in MEK and acetone. Made flexible by the addition of a chemical plasticizer, vinyl caps are not as flexible as rubber caps. (Vinyl caps can be purchased from any of the make-up suppliers.) The edges are very thin and can be melted down with acetone to achieve an even thinner application; as this cap is not rubber, regular make-up can be applied to it.

Foam Latex Caps

A Foam Latex cap is just what it says, latex that is foamed. It has been the industry standard for many years when referring to a prosthetic appliance. However there has been a higher demand for very realistic make-ups and foam latex is now being used to create a realistic bald look. It is very different from the other two, which come in generic sizes. The foam latex cap has to be custom made for each performer and follows the same principles of any other prosthetic appliance. As a matter of fact a rubber bald cap is applied first and then the more realistic foam latex is applied over it. Coloring a foam latex cap is the same as coloring a rubber cap or a prosthetic appliance; both are made of latex. Pax Paint is another product you can paint latex products with. It cannot be purchased pre-mixed; you have to mix it yourself. The ingredients are 40% Pros-aide adhesive, 40% acrylic paint, and 20% matte medium. The nice thing about Pax Paint is you can pre-paint your cap with it long before you ever apply it to the performer. Because it's made with Pros-aide, it is important to powder the paint thoroughly after it is dry.

Rubber Cap Construction

The following is a step-by-step procedure for making a rubber bald cap using Pliatex Mold Rubber and a MUD Bald Cap Form.

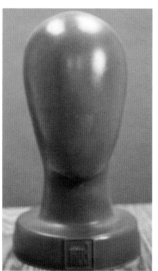

Mud Bald Cap Form.

Step 1
White sponge prior to tearing.

Step 2
First, prepare a white sponge for the application by ripping the end off, so a rough surface is left. This will leave an uneven texture to the surface of the cap.

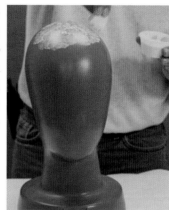

Step 3
Using Pliatex Mold Rubber, apply one layer of rubber to the form. Start at the crown of the Bald Cap Form and work down towards the face and down towards the neck.

Step 4
Be very careful not to allow the sponge to dry out. If the sponge dries out, it will stick to the latex on the Bald Cap Form as it starts to dry.

Step 5
Apply thin even layers. Thin layers will dry much faster than thick ones.

Step 6

Map out your application, making sure latex is applied everywhere.

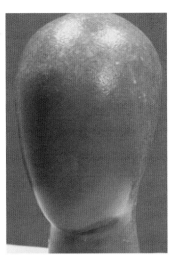

Step 11

We recommend six layers of Pliatex Mold Rubber over the Bald Cap Form. Depending on how thick or thin you make those layers you may need to adjust how many layers you apply.

Step 7

As the latex dries it will begin to turn clear.

Step 12

Once all six layers are complete and the latex is completely dry, take your index finger and roll the edge onto itself. Work all the way around the cap.

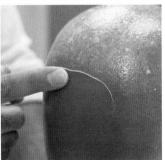

Step 8

Allow the latex to dry thoroughly before continuing. Use a hair dryer to speed up the drying time.

Step 13

Again, six layers may or may not be enough latex. It is intended as a guide. After you have finished your first cap and it is removed you will be able to tell if more or less layers were necessary.

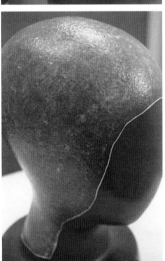

Step 9

Start each layer at the top and work down. Do not rub the latex on, or it will tear the first layer. Apply the latex with a stippling motion, carefully moving the latex around Bald Cap Form.

Step 10

A total of six layers should be applied to the form. Each layer should be applied "inside" the edge of the last layer applied. Try to keep the edges where you think your blending edge will be very thin.

Step14

Powder the entire cap with a powder puff, being very careful to not wrinkle or damage the surface.

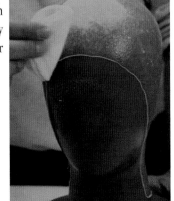

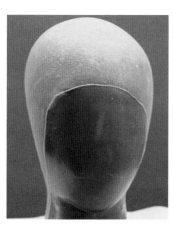

Step 15

The powdered cap. Dust off any loose powder.

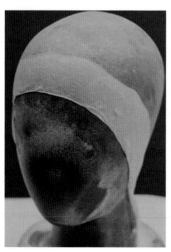

Step 16

Grab the edge by the rolled end and slowly peel the cap back as you powder underneath it.

Step 17

Slowly move around the edge of the cap until two (2) inches of the edge is pulled back, and powdered.

Step 18

Continue around the cap in this fashion, until the cap is completely removed from the edge of the Bald Cap Form. This helps prevent the edges from sticking to each other.

Step 19

Push the brush under the cap along the sides of the cap, leaving a strip down the middle of the Bald Cap Form.

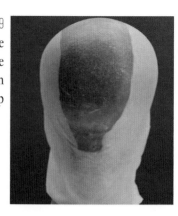

Step 20

Slowly peel off this strip, powdering as you go. By undoing the sides first the center strip comes off easily.

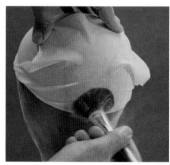

Step 21

Turn the cap inside out and place it back onto the form. Re-powder the inside of the cap with a powder puff and a liberal amount of powder. This is to ensure you didn't miss a spot. This would be a good time to gently pull apart and re-powder any

area of the cap that might have stuck together as you were trying to remove it.

Step 22

The cap is now ready to use! It is recommended you use this cap before attempting to make another cap. A great deal is learned after you have applied the cap you just made.

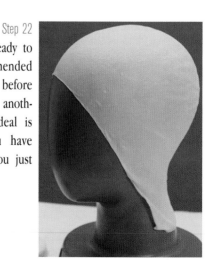

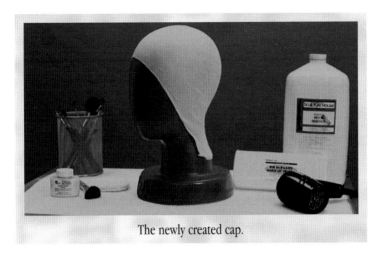

The newly created cap.

Rubber Bald Cap Application

The single most important thing to remember before you start is that this application is going to be fun.

Preparing the Model

Sit the model in a chair that elevates him to a height that is comfortable for you. This application will take about ninety minutes, so standing upright is very important. Have the model sit in an upright position as far back in the chair as possible. He should be wearing a shirt that allows plenty of access to the neck area.

Step 1
Plain water being used to slick the hair back. Combing the hair first will help it not to tangle. Wet the hair using a spray bottle filled with water and comb back, whilst trying to get the hair to lay down as flat as possible.

Step 2
Taking control of the hair is the first challenge of a bald cap. Since this is a rubber cap most hair gels, and hair products in general, will adversely affect the cap and its application. We find just plain water to be most effective when utilizing a rubber cap.

Step 3
The hair slicked back. Do not make the hair overly wet; the excess water can cause you problems later on.

Clean the inside of the Bald Cap of any residue powder or debris by wiping it out with 99% alcohol on a tissue.

Fitting the cap

Contrary to popular belief, size does matter! If you are given a choice, it's better to pick a bald cap that is somewhat small, rather than one that is too big. It is essential to position the cap to fit the crown of the head and lie flat against the nape of the neck. This will alleviate wrinkles at the sides and back of the bald cap. A cap that is too large will require a little cutting and some patching to ensure the proper fit.

A cap that is rotated too far forward will make the back of the cap flare away from the neck. A cap that is rotated too far back will have horizontal wrinkles along the nape of the neck.
Clean the skin with 99% alcohol to ensure the cap will stick to the skin.

Step 1
Slipping the cap on the head. Stretch the bald cap to ensure proper placement on the crown of the head.

Step 2
Positioning the cap so there are no wrinkles at the neck area.

Attaching the Cap

Choosing the right adhesive is just as important as choosing the right size of cap. Of all the choices available Pros-aide seems to work the best. Pros-aide is a contact adhesive that is most effective when applied to both surfaces, allowed to dry and then pressed together. The front anchoring point is the first place to apply adhesive.

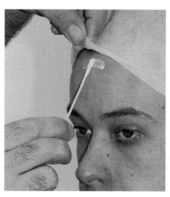

Step 1
Lifting the front edge and applying Pros-aide to the skin and to the cap. Apply Pros-aide to the center of the forehead and to the inside of the cap, allow to dry and then press together. This anchor point will be placed under a lot of pres-

sure, so having a strong bond is essential.

Step 2
Applying Pros-aide to the back of the bald cap for the back anchor point. Make sure both spots of adhesive are completely dry before pressing together. For the back anchoring point tip the model's head back slightly. Applying Pros-aide to the back of the neck, and again to the inside of the cap, allow both sides to dry, then press together.

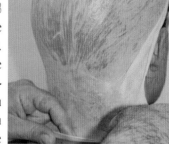

Step 3
Attaching the back of the cap to the back of the neck. Pulling down while the model lifts his chin. By tipping the head back as you glue the cap down you ensure a tight fit. When the model straightens his head the cap will be placed under tension and be wrinkle free.

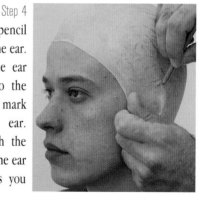

Step 4
Using a make-up pencil make a mark above the ear. Mark right above the ear where it attaches to the head, running the mark down behind the ear. Remember to stretch the bald cap down over the ear and into position as you draw your line.

Step 5
The finished mark with the bald cap in a relaxed position.

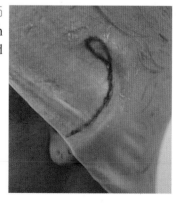

Step 6

Make a small cut along the line. Cut along the marked line, being careful not to create little jagged edges as these may become large tears.

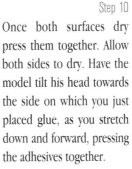

Step 10

Once both surfaces dry press them together. Allow both sides to dry. Have the model tilt his head towards the side on which you just placed glue, as you stretch down and forward, pressing the adhesives together.

Step 7

Run the scissors along the line, as opposed to making cuts. the material is very soft and tears easily. Now, glue the ear down by applying Pros-aide to the skin from the back anchoring point up to the back of the ear.

Step 11

The front of the ear is the next area to be glued. Apply adhesive to the skin from the top of the ear, around the sideburn to the front anchoring point.

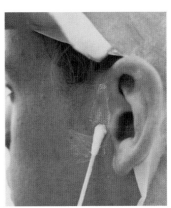

Step 8

A band of adhesive running from the back anchor point to the top of the ear. The adhesive should be applied along the hairline, about 1/2 inch in width. Apply Pros-aide to the cap from the back anchoring point to the back of the ear.

Step 12

And apply the same adhesive to the inside of the cap. We usually make the adhesive spot bigger on the bald cap, providing a little more room to stretch and reposition it if necessary. The dried adhesive will not bond to the hair. Now, apply Pros-aide to the cap from the top of the ear, around the sideburn to the front anchoring point.

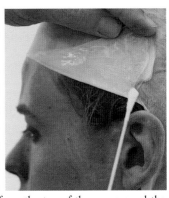

Step 9

Apply a mirror image of the adhesive to the inside of the bald cap, and allow to dry.

Step 13

Pull down and forward to alleviate any wrinkles around the ear, pressing the two dried surfaces together. This is what the finished side of the bald cap should look like. Repeat the steps for attaching the bald-cap around the ear on the other side of the head.

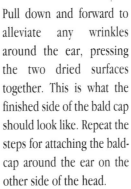

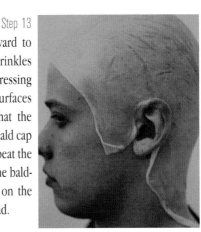

Trimming the Cap

To trim the edge of the cap, use a pair of scissors, first pulling the cap up and out of the adhesive.

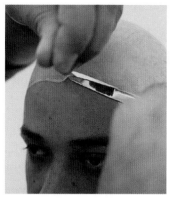

Step 1

Lift up on the edge, pulling the cap out of the adhesive. Trim the edge, then lay the cap back into the glue. Cut away the excess cap and lay the newly trimmed edge back down into the adhesive.

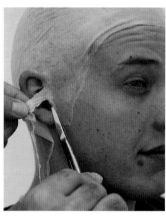

Step 2

Cut every edge of the cap. Do this all the way around the cap. Make sure the edge is jagged and uneven, this will help to blend the edge.

Blending the Cap

There are not many chemicals that easily dissolve rubber. Some make-up artists are using naptha to melt the edge of the rubber cap, which works but naptha (lighter fluid) is a little rough on the skin. Another way to get the edge to blend is to apply something that will build the skin up to the same level as the surface of the cap. Pros-aide once again is the answer, but this time add Cab-o-sil to it to create a thick paste. Cab-o-sil is fumed silica, used to thicken resins, and great care should be taken when handling this product. The silica is lighter than air and can become airborne very easily, which if inhaled can cause problems. It is recommended that you wear a dust mask when handling Cab-o-sil in its powdered form. When the Pros-aide and the Cab-o-sil are combined in a 50/50 ratio it is commonly referred to as Bondo. Bondo is a trade name for a fiberglass product used to fill in dents on a car. This is not the same product we use on people's faces. We use the name Bondo for the Pros-aide/Cab-o-sil combination because it works very much like its namesake.

Step 1

Apply a combination of Cab-o-sil and Pros-aide called Bondo to the edge of the bald cap. Slowly build it up to the desired thickness.

Apply the Bondo to the skin and blend it into the cap. It is very important to keep the Bondo off the cap, because if you apply it to both the skin and the cap you won't actually fix anything, as you would only be making your edge bigger. Bondo is used to fill in the edge created by the cap as it sits on top of the skin. Use a pallet knife to apply the Bondo, starting on the skin, and sweep it up to the edge of the cap without going over. Apply the Bondo all the way around the cap.

The Bondo, once dry, will sometimes leave a smooth surface all the way around the cap. To match the texture of the cap to the skin, tear a white sponge in the same fashion you tore the sponge when you made the cap.

Step 2

Using a torn white sponge stipple latex over the edge of the cap. The texture will match the texture of the cap. Apply the latex over the edge of the cap and onto the skin in the same way you applied it when making the cap. You may need two or three layers to completely cover the edge. Once the latex dries, powder it.

Coloring the Cap

This step of the application is the most critical. If you make a mistake here, even if your application is perfect, your entire cap may not turn out. However, if you make mistakes in the application of the cap, this step could completely save you. First, mix a perfect base match using rubber mask grease paint. It is very important to mix the right base color, because it is the base for the entire make-up. Using a pallet knife spread the base color of RMGP onto the cap. Do not use too much; a little will go a long way. (I use a combination of base color I call base soup.) This combination of colors is applied all over the head.

Step 1

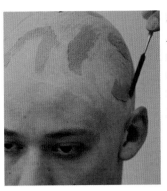

Applying a couple of different shades of base to the cap. Choose colors that match colors in the model's face.

Step 2

Either with a white sponge or a brush, mix the colors on the head. Using a white sponge, stipple the color together blending and moving it over the head.

Step 3

The colors you've applied begin to look spotted and textured, just like real skin.

Step 4

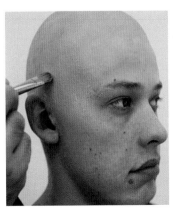

A brush, damp with 99% alcohol, is used to smooth out the edges, and blend the base into the skin. Powder the base with a liberal amount of pigmented powder. You really want to set this base properly so you won't accidentally remove make-up.

Step 5

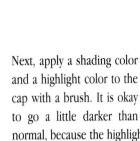

Highlight and shadow being applied.

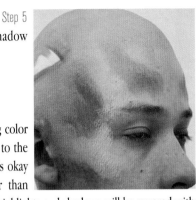

Next, apply a shading color and a highlight color to the cap with a brush. It is okay to go a little darker than normal, because the highlights and shadows will be covered with more base colors. Paint the shadow under the jawbone, beneath the cheekbone, into the temples and onto the forehead. Wherever possible apply the shadow across the edge of the cap; this will help to further blend the edge. The highlight should be placed on top of the cheekbones and along the bone structure that makes up the eye sockets. Powder the highlights and shadows.

Step 6

With an orange stipple sponge, stipple at least 3 different shades of base color onto the cap, a lighter, a darker, and a base match, giving the cap that needed texture; this will also help to soften the highlights and shadows, and aid in blending the edge.

Step 7

Once more, using the orange stipple sponge, apply small amounts of both blue and green mixed with the base color. This will give the bald cap that translucent skin quality. Also, a small amount of mustard yellow may be needed to help the colors blend. Finally, apply a brick color to the cap, to give it the necessary redness of skin. Do not be afraid to use a lot. Both film and TV will remove some of the red so a little more than what seems to be right is desirable. Lightly powder the cap, when finished, with a translucent powder. A small amount is all that is needed.

Bald Cap   Chapter 10

Before   *After*

Vinyl Bald Cap Application:

The vinyl bald cap application is almost identical to the rubber bald cap application with a few exeptions. I have re-written the entire procedure to illustrate the differences.

Preparing the Model

Sit the model in a chair that elevates him/her to a height that is comfortable for you. This application will take about ninety minutes, so standing upright is very important. Have the model sit in an upright position, as far back in the chair as possible. He/she should be wearing a shirt that allows plenty of access to the neck area.

Wet the hair using a spray bottle filled with water, combing back in order to get the hair to lay down as flat as possible. Gafquat is an excellent choice to flatten and control the hair so it will not interfere with the cap application; it can be thinned with water and applied over well combed, wet hair. Additionally, Gafquat can be applied full strength along the hairline with a comb or toothbrush.

Clean the inside of the bald cap of any residue powder or debris by wiping it out with 99% alcohol on a tissue.

Slip cap on the head.

Fitting the cap

The same applies to a vinyl bald cap as it does to a rubber bald cap. If you are given a choice, it's better to pick a bald cap that is somewhat small, rather than one that is too big. It is essential to position the cap to fit the crown of the head and to lie flat against the nape of the neck. This will alleviate wrinkles at the sides and back of the bald cap. A cap that is too large will require a little cutting and some patching to ensure the proper fit. A cap that is rotated too far forward will make the back of the cap flare away from the neck. A cap that is rotated too far back will have horizontal wrinkles along the nape of the neck. Clean the skin with 99% alcohol to ensure that the cap will stick to the skin.

Attaching the Cap

Choosing the right adhesive is just as important as choosing the correct sized cap. Of all the choices available Pros-aide seems to work the best. Pros-aide is a contact adhesive that acts better if it is applied to both surfaces, allowed to dry then pressed together. The front anchoring point is the first place to apply adhesive. Apply Pros-aide to the center of the forehead and to the inside of the cap, allow to dry, and then press together. For the back anchoring point, tip the model's head back slightly, apply Pros-aide to the back of the neck and again to the inside of the cap, allowing both sides to dry, then press together. By tipping the head back as you glue the cap down you ensure a tight fit. When the model straightens his/her head the cap will be placed under tension and wrinkle free.

Next, mark one ear with a make-up pencil as you stretch the bald cap down over the ear. Mark right above the ear where it attaches to the head, then run the mark down behind the ear. Cut along the marked line, being careful not to create little jagged edges; jagged edges may become large tears.

To glue the ear down by applying Pros-aide to the skin from the back anchoring point up to the back of the ear. The adhesive should be applied along the hairline, about 1/2 inch in width. Apply Pros-aide to the cap from the back anchoring point to the back of the ear. Allow both sides to dry. Have the model tilt his head towards the side you placed the glue, as you stretch down and forward, and press the adhesives together.

The front of the ear is the next area to be glued. Apply adhesive to the skin from the top of the ear, around the sideburn to the front anchoring point, then apply Pros-aide to the cap from the top of the ear, around the sideburn to the front anchoring point. Allow both sides to dry, pull down and forward to alleviate any wrinkles around the ear, and press the two surfaces together.

Repeat the steps for attaching the ear, on the other side of the head.

Trimming the Cap

To trim the edge of the cap, use a pair of scissors after first pulling the cap up and out of the adhesive. Cut away the excess cap and lay the newly trimmed edge back down into the adhesive. Do this all the way around the cap.

Blending the Cap

The chemical that is used to dissolve the vinyl is acetone. Acetone is highly volatile, which means it evaporates very quickly. To apply the acetone, use a cotton swab and lightly dab it onto the edge. You must take certain precautions to protect the eyes from the acetone. Simply place a powder puff over the eyes, so nothing can drip down into them. Keep in mind you should not be using enough acetone to drip. An additional way to get the edge to blend is to apply something that will build the skin up to the same level as the surface of the cap. Pros-aide once again is the answer, but this time add Cab-o-sil to it to create a thick paste. Cab-o-sil is fumed silica, used to thicken resins. Great care should be taken when handling Cab-o-sil. The silica is lighter than air and can become airborne very easily, which if inhaled can cause problems; it's a good idea to wear a dust mask when handling it in its powdered form. When the Pros-aide and the Cab-o-sil are combined in a 50/50 ratio it is commonly referred to as Bondo. Bondo is a trade name for a fiberglass product used to fill in dents on a car. This is not the same product we use on people's faces. We use the name Bondo for the Pros-aide/Cab-o-sil combination because it works very much like its namesake. Apply the Bondo to the skin and blend it into the cap. It is very important to keep the Bondo off the cap, because if you apply it to both the skin and the cap you won't actually fix anything, you would only be making your edge bigger. Bondo is used to fill in the edge created by the cap as it sits on top of the skin. Use a pallet knife to apply the Bondo starting on the skin and sweeping it up to the edge of the cap without going over. Apply the Bondo all the way around the cap. The Bondo once dry will sometimes leave a smooth surface all the way around the cap. To match the texture of the cap to the skin, apply plastic sealer over the edge of the cap and onto the skin. You may need two or three layers to completely cover the edge.

Coloring the Cap

This step of the application is the most critical. If you make a mistake here, even if your application is perfect, your entire cap may not turn out. However, if you make mistakes in the application of the cap this step could completely save you. First, mix a perfect base match using regular cream make-up. It is very important to mix the right base color, because it is the base for the entire make-up. Using a pallet knife, spread the base color onto the cap, not using too much; a little will go a long way. With a white sponge, stipple the color together, blending and moving it over the head, then use a large brush that is damp with 99% alcohol to blend the edge of the color into the skin. Powder the base with a liberal amount of pigmented powder. You must set this base properly so you will not accidentally remove make-up.

With a brush, apply a shading color and a highlight color to the cap. It is okay to go a little darker than normal, because more base colors will be applied over the highlight and shadow. Paint the shadow under the jawbone, beneath the cheekbone, into the temples and onto the forehead. Wherever possible, apply the shadow across the edge of the cap; this will help to further blend the edge. The highlight should be placed on top of the cheekbones and along the bone structure that makes up the eye sockets. Powder the highlights and shadows.

With an orange stipple sponge, stipple at least 3 different shades of base color onto the cap, one lighter, another darker, and a base match, which will give the cap that needed texture. It will also help soften the highlights and shadows, and of course help blend the edge. Powder again.

Once more, using the orange stipple sponge, apply small amounts of both blue and green mixed with the base color. This will give the bald cap that translucent skin quality. Also a small amount of mustard yellow may be needed to help the colors blend. Finally, apply a brick color to the cap, to give it the necessary redness of skin. Do not be afraid to use a lot. Both film and tv will remove a little of the red so slightly more than what seems to be right is desirable. Lightly powder the cap when finished, with a translucent powder. A small amount is all that is needed.

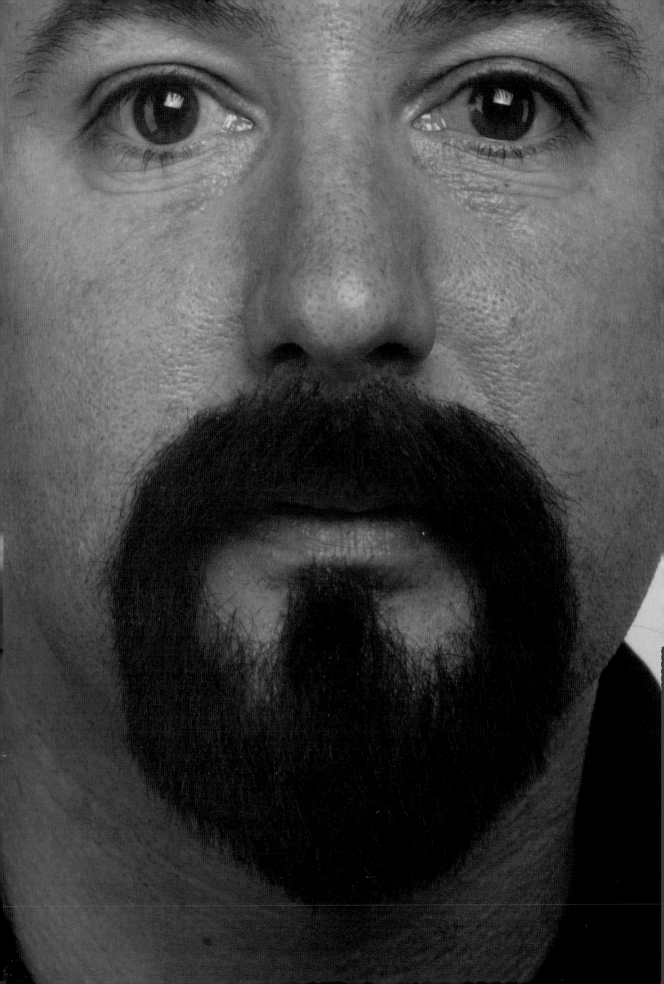

Chapter 11

Beards & Mustaches

Introduction to Beards & Mustaches

The definition of "hair work" is the application of hair to the face or body. There are two main methods of hair application, loose hair applied by hand, or the application of a ventilated hairpiece. Several types of hair are used, the first being, of course, human hair, then there is yak hair, crepe wool a.k.a. sheep's wool, and synthetic hair. Human hair comes in two versions: Asian, the most common, and European. European is the more expensive, only because there is less of it on the market. Yak hair is from a yak and is slightly coarser than human hair. Yak is a little less expensive than human hair. Crepe wool isn't hair at all, it is wool in long strands that simulate hair, mainly used in theater and for the purpose of learning. It is a great tool for learning as it is so inexpensive, about $8.00 for four ounces. Synthetic hair is a plastic product, typically used for wigs, and is also one of the lowest priced available.

For most productions, a combination of human and yak hair are mixed together to create hair that looks real with good body. Both usually come on a weft and are about 10 to 12 inches in length. The hair is sewn to the weft and needs to be prepared before you can apply it. Cut the hair away from the weft and lay all the hair going the same direction. There is a root and a point to the hair and you want all of the hair to be piled in the same direction. Around each hair, this applies to both human and yak hair, is what is called the cuticle layer. This cuticle layer, under a microscope, looks like scales. What this actually means is if the root and point are mixed up, the hair will become easily matted. The hair also must be crimped, especially if you are using it as facial hair. A crimping iron can be used on both types of hair, but an old fashioned pleating machine that has been wired to heat up works the best. Now, where do you get an old fashioned pleating machine? There are a few companies that have them for rent, Frends in North Hollywood, for example, being one of them. It is also possible to purchase the hair pre-crimped from various suppliers.

For synthetic hair, there is very little preparation required. You purchase it either straight or crimped and it is ready for use. There is no cuticle layer to worry about, and it comes in 36 to 48 inch lengths. Synthetic hair is quite difficult to apply and is really only used in those situations where a long beard is necessary.

Crepe wool comes in a variety of colors, none of which are very realistic, and can be mixed to produce a halfway decent look. Try not to use straight black or white as both are very stark, making it almost impossible to achieve a natural look. Crepe wool is, on average, between 6 to 8 inches in length and a braided yard will usually yield approximately 4 ounces of hair.

Hand laid hair versus lace appliances

A lace hairpiece or appliance is the fastest way to get hair glued to the face, but it is less comfortable than hand laid hair. Hand laying hair is quite time consuming and very hard to match on a daily basis, whereas a lace beard can be reapplied on a daily basis and will match perfectly. Continuity is easier with a lace appliance. Lace is more expensive so, in the world of low budget projects, hand laid hair is still used quite extensively. Comfort is sometimes an issue; if an actor is really bothered by the scratchiness of the lace then you may have to resort to laying hair. Keep in mind that even if you do use lace hairpieces, you still need to hand lay the edge of the beard to create the most realistic look.

Preparation of Crepe Wool

The following is a step-by-step procedure for properly preparing crepe wool. Only crepe wool needs this procedure done to it as all the other available hairs can be purchased already prepared for you. For the purpose of learning how to apply hair, crepe wool is an inexpensive alternative to using human or yak hair.

The crepe wool as it comes from the package. This type of hair is not really hair at all; it is actually wool woven into a braid.

Step 1

To prepare crepe wool for use it must first be unraveled from the strings. Lightly pull on one end of a braid; the wool will separate slightly from the strings. Now, unravel the strings away from the wool. (If you pull too far the hair and strings will become knotted.)

Step 2

To keep the hair and strings from knotting as you pull them, simply cut off the excess strings as you go. Continue till the strings are completely removed from the braid. Once the strings have been removed you need to eliminate approximately 60% of the curl from the wool. You can completely remove all the curl from the wool, but this may result in a very flat look.

Step 3

A steam iron can be used to alleviate the curl by stretching the crepe wool across an ironing board, removing about 60% of the curl, then taping or pinning the wool in place. Next, iron the wool to take away the curl, so that when the tape or pins are removed the preferred amount of curl will be omitted. Steam is really the fastest way to straighten the wool out. A clothes steamer or a teapot can be used for this.

Step 4

Simply hang the wool strand over a steady stream of steam; the wool will slowly relax as you hold it there. Be careful not to leave it too long or the hair will completely straighten. Again, the goal is to remove about 60% of the curl.

Step 5

The straighter the crepe wool is, the easier it will be to apply. Unfortunately, in most cases, the straighter the crepe wool is, the less realistic it will look when applied to the face. One notable exception is Asian facial hair. This type of hair tends to be very straight requiring almost all of the curl to be removed before application. Another exception to the whole straightening process is the application of African-American facial hair. This type of facial hair is extremely curly, therefore no curl is removed from the braid before application.

Step 6

Once the end is straightened you can safely grab the end of the wool without accidently burning yourself; hold the wool in the stream of steam, then as it straightens, move the wool along the opening of the steamer, slowly relaxing the curl of the entire braid.

Step 7

You can see, as the wool passes through the steam, it relaxes, allowing you to use it right away. Do not stretch the wool braid as you hold it in the stream of steam.

The completely steamed wool. Approximately 60% of the curls has been removed.

Step 8

The next procedure is to pull the straightened braid of crepe wool apart. Hold the wool from one end and gently begin pulling from the other end. The wool fibers will separate into 6 to 8 inch pieces.

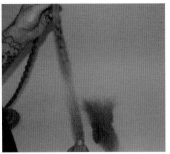

Step 9

Continue to pull from both ends of the braid until you have a pile of wool that will be ready to run through a hair hackle.

Step 10

Once all the hair is separated into six to eight inch lengths, then you need to finish preparing it by continuing to pull from the ends.

Step 11

Hold the hair at one end with a good grip then pull from the other. This will further separate the individual strands of wool, enhancing the look of the hair. Return the hair to the bundle then pull it again. Repeat this procedure until the wool looks fluffy and even.

Step 12

A close-up of the hair being held; the forefinger and thumb are holding the bulk of the hair. If you grip the hair too tightly you will not be able to pull it apart properly.

The finished hair is piled up then wrapped in a paper towel for safe keeping.

A Hackle and its Use

A hackle is a piece of wood or metal with a series of closely placed pins, set up in rows, that are used like a giant comb to de-tangle most types of hair.

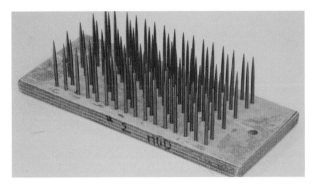

The hackle.

Step 1

The hackle should be clamped or taped securely to the edge of the counter. Always cover the hackle with a piece of balsa wood, a tissue box, or anything that will prevent you from accidentally injuring yourself.

Step 2

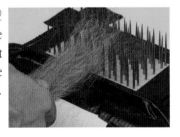

Hair is run through the hackle to remove short hairs and tangles from the pile of hair being prepared.

Step 3

Hold onto the center of the hair with a good grip; you do not want any hair escaping your grip as it is detangled.

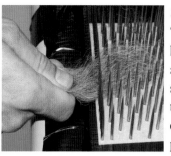

Step 4

To properly use the hackle, begin by carefully placing approximately one inch of a small amount of hair into the hackle. Do this very carefully and slowly as the pins in the hackle are quite sharp, and if you rush you may become impaled upon the hackle. Holding the hair firmly, now pull it towards you, through the hackle.

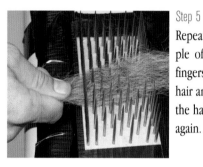

Step 5

Repeat this process a couple of times. moving your fingers down the length of hair an inch or so, then run the hair through the hackle again.

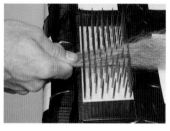

Step 6

Keep moving your fingers down an inch then run the hair through the hackle until you reach the center of the chunk of hair; turn the hair around and repeat the entire process once again with the other half of the hair.

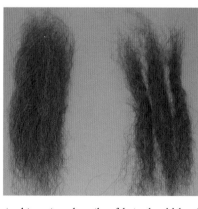

The hair on the left is hackled, but the hair on the right is not. Hackling the hair first allows for easier application.

At this point, the pile of hair should be de-tangled and all the short hairs removed. Continue until all of the hair needed has been run through the hackle. As hair is run through the hackle, short hairs and tangles will build up in the pins. When the short hairs and tangles begin to interfere with the hair being prepared they should be removed from the hackle and set aside. Take the

short hair and tangled pieces and pull them apart end from end, until the hair is straightened out again and can be run through the hackle. You may repeat this procedure until all of the hair has been straightened and separated into piles of different lengths. Never throw away any of the hair that is left behind in the hackle. Even the left over fuzz can be used for beard stubble.

Proper Cutting Technique

Applying hair breaks down into a few simple steps. Properly cutting the hair is key to a good application.

Step 1

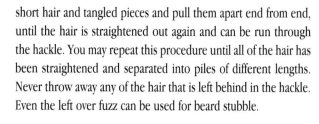

Grip the hair properly. Hold the hair between your thumb and forefinger. Hold the hair tightly, and once you start this process do not let go until you place it on the face.

Step 2

Comb the hair against a leg, this will make sure the hair is run through the comb, allowing it to flair out properly.

Step 3

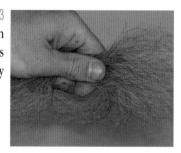

Hold the hair so you can comb all of it. Any tangles you put into the hair may cause problems later on.

Step 4

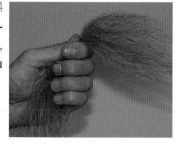

Hold the hair in the position you want to apply it, visualizing the shape you want it to have.

Step 5

Then cut the top edge off hair. The shape is not important, round, square, or triangular, any will do; during your regular applications you may find yourself doing combinations of different cuts.

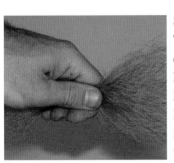

Step 6

The amount of hair sticking out from your finger directly relates to how thick the hair is applied. The more hair sticking out, the thinner the application, while the closer the end of the hair is held the thicker it will be. Careful, you may end up with carpeting.

Step 7

Cut the sides down to help control the amount of hair on them. Cut one side down, then the other.

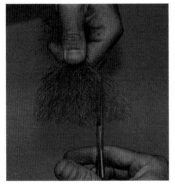

Step 8

Notice how we turn the hair so when it is cut the shavings fall away without getting stuck in it.

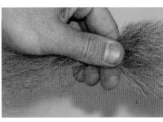

Step 9

The hair is now ready to be beveled.

Step 10

Turn the hair sideways holding it in the direction in which you want it to grow; in this case in a downward direction.

Step 11

Next, hold the scissors parallel to the face as you cut up the backside of the hair. This is called beveling.

Step 12

Make sure all the cuttings fall away from the piece you are going to apply to the face.

The finished bevel cut ready to be applied.

Hand Laid Hair

The art form of hand laying hair to an actor's face is slowly being forgotten. Many make-up artists feel the process is completely different from any other type of make-up they may be asked to do. Some even think this should be the job of the hairdresser. As the make-up artist you are responsible for the total look of the actor. You would not want someone else applying hair, particularly in the eyebrow area, over your finely detailed prosthetic appliance.

Typically, hand-laying hair is not used in most productions because of the difficulty in matching it on a daily basis. Continuity being such a large concern has led us to use pre-made lace appliances for most of our hair needs. However, because hand laying hair is relatively inexpensive it is still utilized for background performers and low budget projects.

Applying hair to an actor is not particularly difficult, it just requires some practice. Keeping your station and tools clean and organized is a huge part of a successful application, then working out a repeatable system for each piece you glue on.

A couple of final suggestions – do not use too much hair and remember you want the hair to essentially stand on end, with only the ends of the hair stuck in the glue.

The model ready for a hand laid beard, his face completely clean of any oil or make-up.

Step 2 A

Step 2 B

Fold the hair in half making a loop and then cut it on the loop. Because the hair is not a uniform length, if you tried to apply the hair without cutting it you would find that most of the hair would fall out. We are cutting it in half because we are going to do a short beard.

Step 3

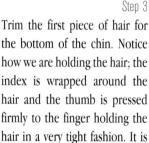

Trim the first piece of hair for the bottom of the chin. Notice how we are holding the hair; the index is wrapped around the hair and the thumb is pressed firmly to the finger holding the hair in a very tight fashion. It is important to remember once you have the hair in this position to not let go until the hair is stuck to the face or you will have to re-trim the hair every time you re-position it.

Step 4

Hold the hair up to the chin to measure and see what needs to be trimmed. Cut away all unwanted hair and be sure to bevel the hair that is going to stick to the face.

Step 1

We will be using crepe wool for our beard. As previously discussed the wool comes in predetermined lengths of about six to eight inches. So take a small amount to start with and make sure you comb through it thoroughly before using the hair.

Step 5

Do a final test fit of the hair prior to adding glue. For the bottom of the chin the hair should be growing slightly forward so make sure you apply the hair going in this direction. As you hold the hair up to the face be careful not to smash it into the face.

Positioning the hair like this will allow you to see exactly where you will need to apply the adhesive.

Step 6

Using a silicone adhesive, dip your cotton swab first into the thinner and then into the adhesive; this will help keep the adhesive thin as it goes on the skin. Depending on which brand of adhesive you choose will depend on how much working time you will have to get the hair stuck to the face.

Step 7

Once the area is coated in glue, gently press the hair into it and hold until dry. The nice thing about silicone adhesives is their ability to dry quickly. You can use the back of the wooden cotton swab to help press the hair into the adhesive.

Step 8

Once the adhesive is dry and the hair stuck to the face you can relax your death grip on the hair. Using the pick side of a comb, carefully pick through the hair to remove any hair that is not stuck in the adhesive.

Step 9

Notice the thinness of the hair left on the chin. This is perfect; we will be adding more in front of this piece and we want to be able to see into the hair. If it gets too thick the beard will look fake.

Step 10

The next piece will go in front of the last piece. Start by combing the hair out and notice we are holding it exactly the same way as the last. Combing the hair removes any small pieces of hair that may cause you problems later on and it also ensures that all the hairs are going in the right direction.

Step 11

Measure the hair to the chin and then trim the piece into the shape you want. Remember to bevel cut the hair so that the hair will be growing in the right direction.

Step 12

Apply adhesive to the top of the chin, being very careful not to get the glue in the first piece of hair. As soon as the adhesive is applied, press the hair into the glue. You want the hair to look like it is growing out of the skin, so carefully lay the edges into the adhesive.

Step 13

Use the back of the cotton swab to gently push the hair down. Once the hair is stuck and the adhesive dry you can release the hair. Again, use the pick side of a comb to gently comb out the stray hairs.

Step 14

The next piece is the small piece that goes under the lower lip. We have combed, measured, trimmed, and beveled this piece in the exact same way as the last piece. Using a little less adhesive than the last piece and carefully applying it so it doesn't get on the lower piece.

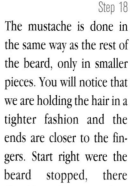

Step 18

The mustache is done in the same way as the rest of the beard, only in smaller pieces. You will notice that we are holding the hair in a tighter fashion and the ends are closer to the fingers. Start right were the beard stopped, there should not be any gap between them.

Step 15

Press the hair into the glue and use the cotton swab to stick down any hair that is not touching the adhesive. Comb through it in the same fashion as the others.

Step 19

Start by the corners of the mouth and work inward. Apply a piece on the right side then on the left, moving from side to side for each piece. This will allow for a more even application.

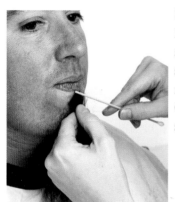

Step 16

In this photograph we are illustrating how to properly measure a piece. We hold the hair in the direction of the hair growth and we are holding the scissors to show how much hair we will have to cut off.

Step 20

Work until the hair meets in the middle under the nose. Working in this area can be a problem for the actor so take special care not to tickle the nose with a lot of excess hair.

Step 17

This piece was adhered and followed the same process we have been talking about with each application. If you can stay neat and clean and perfect your process; namely, comb, measure, cut, bevel, apply the hair, and remove strays, then you will do amazing beards.

Step 21

Now that the hair is all applied, it must be trimmed into a normal beard. Start with the mustache and trim the hair back to the upper lip. You should only trim the center-most part, making sure you are not cutting the side over the corners of the mouth.

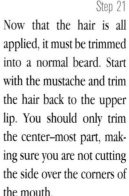

Step 22

To cut the sides over the corners of the mouth hold the scissors close to parallel to the skin, trimming in a downward motion.

Step 23

Now shape perimeter of the beard, using you fingers or a comb to pull out the long sections of hair.

Step 24

Keeping the scissors parallel to the area you are cutting will help prevent accidentally taking out a chunk of the beard.

Step 25

Use tweezers to remove any stray hairs form the beard and from the surface of the skin. We recommend you tweezing between every piece you apply.

The finished beard; note how you can still see skin showing through the hair.

Floating a Beard

The phrase "floating a beard" refers to the process of removing a beard from a toughie head. The beard may also be called a plastic beard. The reason for this is because there is no lace used in this type of appliance, only a plastic spray.

Hair is applied to a toughie head with either spirit gum or a silicone adhesive. The hair is applied typically in the shape of a beard, but just about any shape can be done. The hair is trimmed to a desired length and dressed accordingly with curling irons.

The beard is then sprayed with Krylan's Crystal Clear Acrylic Coating from a distance of 12-15 inches away. After ten minutes, remove the beard with a cotton swab dipped in acetone. Apply the acetone to the toughie head immediately above the upper hairline. As the acetone runs between the block and the beard, it will dissolve the adhesive and release the beard. It is a slow process of carefully dripping the acetone down the front of the toughie head, but with a little patience the beard will be totally removed. Keep in mind, when removing a beard made this way from a person, 99% alcohol should be used instead of the acetone; it will take a little longer but will be much safer and gentler for the performer. Once the beard is removed from the form, spray more acrylic coating to the back of it. This beard is now ready to be applied to a performer. It can be re-used over and over as long as you take special care in removing it each time.

Lace Piece Ventilating

Ventilating is the process of hand knotting individual hairs to a piece of lace. This is done to simulate a beard, mustache, or hair growth. The lace is cut and trimmed into a desired shape and hair is then hand knotted to it, creating a re-usable hair appliance. Human, yak, and synthetic hair are commonly used in this type of lace appliance. The only limitation with synthetic hair is it can not be curled with the Marcel iron and oven

Step 6

Spin the needle wrapping the end of the strand around it

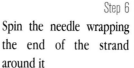

Step 7

Then pull through the loop.

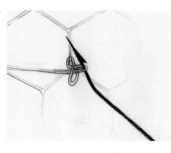

Step 8

The completed knot of hair.

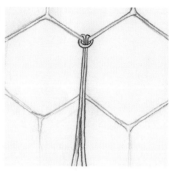

Step 1

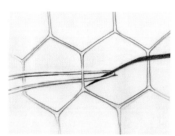

The first step is to push the needle through a hole and then back out through another hole in the lace. Hook a single strand of hair with the needle.

Step 2

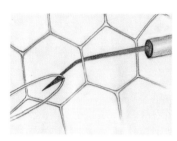

Turn the needle sideways as you pull the single strand of hair through the lace.

Step 3

Push the needle forward once it clears the lace. The needle is still looped by the hair.

Step 4

Push the needle through until you are close to the hair that has not passed through the lace yet.

Step 5

Then hook the strand of hair that has not passed through the lace yet.

Dressing a lace Beard

Before applying a lace beard to the actor it typically needs to be dressed, which means the beard needs to be trimmed and curled to give it a more natural appearance. A lace beard can be used multiple times, meaning that it will need to be curled daily.

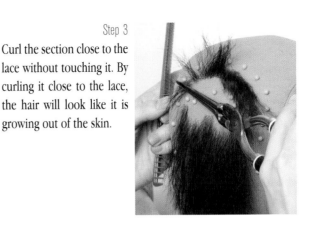

Step 3

Curl the section close to the lace without touching it. By curling it close to the lace, the hair will look like it is growing out of the skin.

The beard and mustache properly pinned to a wig block. Even though the hair is wavy it still needs to be curled to give the beard body. The tools you will need for this process are a comb, scissors, and a small curling Marcel iron and oven.

Step 4

Trim the excess hair to finish grooming the mustache.

Step 1

Test the iron on a piece of tissue to make sure it is not too hot for the hair. If it is too hot it will burn the tissue, leaving a burn or brown mark. If the iron is too cool it will not curl the hair.

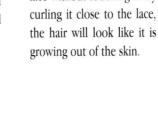

Step 5

The beard is done in the same way the mustache was separated. The beard will be separated from top to bottom as well as from left to right.

Step 2

Separate the mustache into smaller sections to allow for easy access to the individual sections. Each section of hair will need to be curled towards the lip.

Step 6

Again, work as close to the lace without touching it and make sure you are creating enough curl.

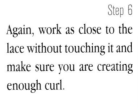

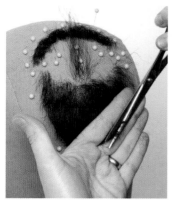

Step 7

Trim any excessively long hairs; use your fingers as a guide to keep the hair in the beard uniform.

Step 9

Trim away the excess lace with scissors. If this lace beard is a rental beard then you will not be able to trim the lace. Be careful not to trim away too much of the lace.

Step 8

You can reach in at any point and add more curl if necessary.

The finished beard and mustache ready to be applied to the actor.

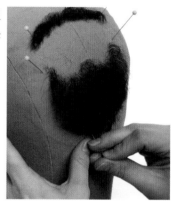

Notes:

Applying a Lace Beard

The best part about using a lace beard is its ease and speed of application. Being able to reuse it over and over runs a close second. The end result is the same with every beard we do; you want the actor to look like they have a beard. Depending on budget and the amount of time you have before you shoot will depend on whether you use a lace appliance or you have to hand lay a beard.

We have chosen the same model so you can see the difference between a hand laid beard and one that is pre-made on lace.

The model prior to having the beard applied.

Step 1
Test fit the beard to the actor to make sure you know where and how it is going to fit the face.

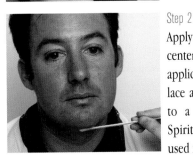

Step 2
Apply silicone adhesive to the center of the chin area. The application of adhesive for a lace appliance is very similar to a prosthetic appliance. Spirit Gum could also be used for a lace application.

Step 3
Press the beard into the adhesive, being careful not to stick the hair into it as well. Stretch the beard into position.

Step 4
Pull back on the unglued area and apply more adhesive; apply only enough to cover the area you are trying to adhere.

Step 5
Press the lace into the new adhesive area while turning the cotton swab around to allow you to lightly tap the edges of the lace into the adhesive.

Step 6
The same procedure is applied to each side of the beard. Remember to stretch the lace lightly to ensure a good fit. Also, you can have the actor hold open his mouth slightly to help area you are adhering.

Step 7
The corner of the mouth is the last area to attach. To ensure a proper application work from side to side so the beard goes on straight.

Step 8
Test fit the mustache to the upper lip and note how it will fit to the beard.

Step 9
Start in the center of the lip area, apply adhesive just in the center and just enough to give you a good adhesion point and small enough to allow for adjustment of the position of the mustache.

Step 10
Lift up on the mustache and apply adhesive right next to last adhesive spot. Then lay the lace into the tacky adhesive. Remember to work on both side of the mustache, alternating from one side to the other to ensure a straight application.

Step 11
Lift up on the corner of the mustache to apply more adhesive; you may need for the actor to open their mouth again to allow the lace to lie down in the adhesive.

Step 12
If any of the hair has gone a little flat you may need to re-curl. Use a metal comb to protect the actor from the hot iron and curl the same way as when you were dressing it.

Step 13

Mustache wax can be used to help the hair keep its curl and shape. Apply a little to a pallet and work it into a make-up brush.

Step 14
Apply the wax over the hair with a brush or your fingers. If the hair was a little longer you could shape it with the wax.

The finished lace beard applied to our actor.

Chapter 12

Bruises

Bruise Progression

Bruises are one of the most common types of special make-up effects done by the make-up artist. They are also open to a wide variety of interpretations. Since every person on the planet bruises a little differently from every other person on the planet, we have found bruising to be highly subjective. So what we will be talking about in this section is the typical and the norm. Remember, every time you do a bruise it will be somewhat different with each interpretation varying also.

Typical Station set-up for minor injuries.

To do bruises properly, you first must understand why skin bruises and what causes all the different colors. Bruising is caused by internal bleeding, when the skin is hit hard enough for the capillaries in it to break. Redness, which is caused by the blood under the skin, shows first, then as the blood begins to coagulate it will turn maroon. As the blood stands, over time, it will darken becoming more blue/purple, and sometimes black.

As the bruise begins to "heal", the areas where the highest concentration of blood are will turn a brownish /bluish color, while the area immediately around the dark patches of skin becomes yellow.

Fresh Bruise

To create a bruise with make-up is relatively simple. Subtlety is everything when doing a bruise. I prefer using a flat brush, smashed to flare all the hairs out. An orange or a black stipple sponge can be used, however these seemingly leave a very even pattern on the skin. Spread a dark red color onto a pallet, in such a way that the brush will pick up the color evenly.

Model before bruising is applied.

Step 1

Stippling a mixture of Lake Red and #79 from the Mud Palette. Creating the effect of broken capillaries.

Step 2

Stipple the dark red color on the area you want to create the bruise. Apply the color lightly, allowing the skin to show through the color.

Step 3

The principals of highlight and shadow are present in every form of make-up you will do, even in a bruise.

Step 4

Using the maroon (Lake Red) as a shadow, and stipple it over the dark red.

Step 5

This will create areas of swelling and will also simulate the worst damaged areas with the most blood.

Step 6

These same steps can be applied to any area, such as the corner of the mouth.

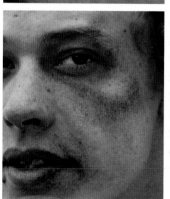

Step 7

Stippling a blue/purple onto the maroon to deepen the shadows slightly - you will not need much of this color.

Step 8

An actual highlight is not used - the natural skin color is the highlight. However, the skin is usually red all over, so leaving it untouched may appear odd.

Step 9

Taking a small amount of red from the palette.

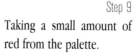

Step 10

A light red stain can now be applied to the highlights to give that skin area color; caution - do not darken that area too much, you will not have any highlight left.

Step 11

Yellow and green can be used lightly in this bruise. Avoid using too much or the bruise will begin to look like an old one.

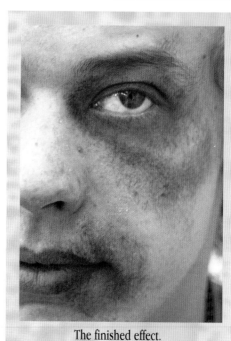

The finished effect.

Aged Bruise

To create a healing bruise, use the same techniques as before, however your colors will be a little different. An old bruise consists more of dried blood under the skin with a faint hint of yellow around it.

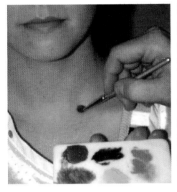

Step 1

Stipple on a yellowish/green color in an uneven pattern. The yellow/green should be used in the same manner in which you applied the dark red color, again allowing the skin to show through the make-up.

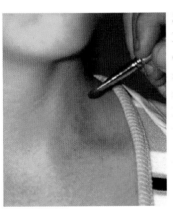

Step 2

Now stipple brownish/blue over the yellow/green in the areas that are most damaged and which would have had the most blood. This time do not shadow with the dark color because the bruise is healing and would no longer be swollen.

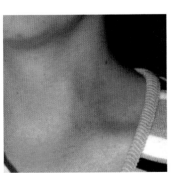

Step 3

Use a Teal Professional Pencil to add that faint blue/green color often found in healing bruises.

Scrapes and Scratches

The following is a very simple effect created with the use of color to give the illusion of depth. Scrapes and scratches can be achieved with wax or as a prosthetic, but in this case we will just use color. Drag a dark red color across the skin, in a straight line, with a black stipple sponge. The lines created by the sponge should taper off in both directions. Then, with a thin brush, paint on very thin black lines over the dark red color, again tapering the ends of the black lines. Do several black lines into the dark red color, but make them various lengths, placing them in different areas. Remember to keep the lines of red and the lines of black running in the same direction as each other; finally, add a small amount of liquid blood to each of the black lines.

The model without any make-up, which will help the overall injury look.

Step 1

Using a coarse black stipple sponge and a combination of two red colors to create a deep blood red. Drag the dark red color across the face in even straight movements. Try to keep the red lines intense in some areas and lighter in others.

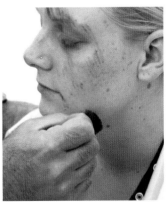

Step 2

Remember to keep the scrape going in one direction; it helps to sell it as a real injury. You may need to use a clean side of the sponge to drag in the opposite direction. This will keep little dots of red from forming where you started your scrape.

Step 3

Use a maroon to deepen a few of the areas. The darker color helps to add irritation to the area. Do not cover the entire red area with the maroon color; add it in small amounts while dragging the color the same way you did the first red.

Step 4

With a small brush, paint ultra thin black lines into the most injured looking areas of the red. The black lines are going to represent the small cuts in the skin. We use black because it will add depth to the cut.

The finished look of the scrape; she looks like she just fell off her bicycle.

Step 5

Blood is applied over each black line and over some of the red lines to finish the effect. Blood could be applied with the black sponge, however, be careful not to over do it.

Notes:

Chapter 13

Tattoos

Tattoos are a fairly easy proposition, even if you have no formal background in drawing, with several ways to approach them. The simplest tattoo is the sticker style, while the freehand drawn style is the hardest one to do and match on a daily basis. (Usually each tattoo comes with a complete set of instructions.)

Freehand Drawn Tattoo

The most difficult thing to accomplish and match on a daily basis, is to freehand draw the tattoo on the actor. Using a taupe make-up pencil, sketch the tattoo as desired. A black make-up pencil is used to finalize the design into a tattoo, followed by the use of a Teal Professional Pencil over the black to create that aged look to the tattoo. (The same effect can be achieved with tattoo inks made by the many manufacturers.) The inks can also be used to color your tattoo. The advantage to the tattoo inks is they dry and will not rub off until removed with 99% alcohol. Powder the tattoo completely with a pigmented powder to finish it. The next series of figures illustrates how to sketch out your design and then darken it. The problem with this process is you have to go over the design three times. On a side note, you could use KD 151's tattoo pens to complete the tattoo. You would still use the taupe pencil to sketch out the design, however you could then use KD 151's aged ink pencil in either 50% or 75% to create the aged look of a tattoo, instead of using the black and teal pencils. An added bonus is the tattoo pens will not rub off.

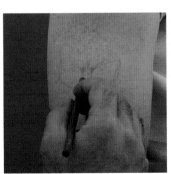

Step 1
Lightly sketch the design with a taupe make-up pencil. Slowly add in elements.

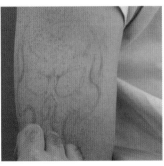

Step 2
Shading with the pencil and wrapping up the design

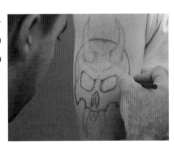

Step 3
The finished design.

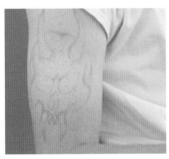

Step 4
Add black with a make-up pencil. Use the black to finalize the shape.

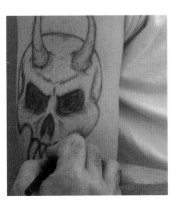

Step 5
Darken in the eyes and nose. Darken shadows and add details.

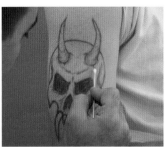

Step 6

Clean off any taupe lines not being used.

Step 7

Use the teal make-up pencil to age the lines.

Step 8

The teal is used on the shadows to soften the edges, as well as, to age the color.

Step 9

Powder the pencil lines. Dust off the excess powder.

Step 10

Completed freehand drawn tattoo.

Tinsley Tattoo

A plastic transfer style tattoo is very similar to a sticker. You can buy a Tinsley tattoo either from your local make-up supplier in the form of a predetermined design, or you can buy directly from the Tinsley company, and they will use whatever artwork you provide. The nice thing about these types of tattoos is their ease in application and once they are applied you do not have to color them. Continuity on this type of tatto is very simple. It is applied with water and removed with any oil based make-up remover. These tattoos are usually full color and come in a wide variety of shapes and sizes. However, this type of tattoo may look shiny when applied. You can control the shine with a small amount of powder or mortician's wax. Simply use a finger to pat the wax over the surface of the sticker.

The off-the-shelf style tattoo made by Tinsley Tattoos.

Step 1

Trim as close to the tattoo as possible with a pair of scissors.

Step 2

Trimming around the tattoo allows the tattoo to easily conform around the area you are applying it to. Next, remove the protective plastic cover off the front of the tattoo.

Step 3

Apply to a clean dry surface. Press firmly to the skin and hold.

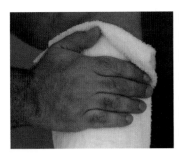

Step 4

Press a damp towel to the back of the tattoo and hold there for several seconds. Allow the water to penetrate the paper backing and soak thru to the tattoo.

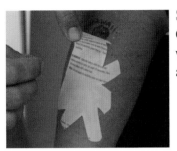

Step 5

Once the tatto is sufficiently wet, slowly peel the paper away.

Step 6

Carefully peeling the paper without removing the tattoo.

The finished tattoo.

Transfer Tattoo

A good alternative to both these types of tattoos is the transfer tattoo. Reel Creations manufactures quality tattoos that can be transferred to the skin, however you may find that you have to use one of their existing designs. It may be possible to contact Reel Creations directly and have an original design made in the same fashion. Another way to create a transfer tattoo is to have someone design a tattoo on paper for you or copy an existing piece of art work, photocopying the art work several times. Turn the art work upside down on a light box and trace the image with an inkblot pencil, called "A Bottle of Ink In a Pencil" onto newsprint paper. It is then applied in the same fashion as the next tattoo except that to transfer it to the skin you would use water instead of 99% alcohol. This pencil is available in most art and make-up supply stores and can be used directly on the skin with water. The transfer tattoo is not designed as a stand-alone application. In both cases it requires you to either go over them with make-up pencils or tattoo pens from KD 151.

Step 1

Cut as close to the tattoo as possible, this will help the tatto to conform to the contours of the skin.

Step 2

You will need 99% alcohol, a powder puff, and the transfer.

Step 3

Dampen the powder puff with alcohol then use it to rub a small amount of alcohol onto the skin. Press the transfer to the skin.

Step 4

Press the puff to the back of the transfer, completely wetting it out. Using too much alcohol will cause the ink on the transfer to run.

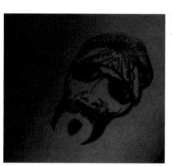

Step 5

Allow the alcohol to dry, then peel off the transfer.

Step 6

The transfered image.

Step 7

Make-up pencils, tattoo inks, or tattoo pens can be used to color this tattoo. Both Reel Creations and Skin Illustrator make wonderful tattoo inks in a pallette form or in a liquid form.

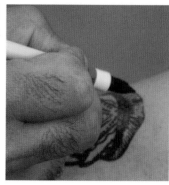

Step 9

Aged Ink 75% is a black color with a little blue tint.

Step 10

Use the pen to fill in and touch up all the line work of the tattoo.

Step 11

A red tattoo pen is used to color the head band in the tattoo. We found the pens very easy to use and very durable.

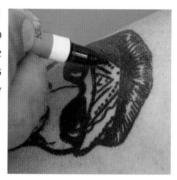

Step 12

Powder the tatto with a little pigmented powder.

Step 8

We are going to use KD 151's tattoo pen, Aged Ink 75%.

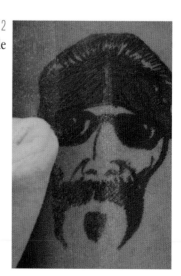

The finished transfer tattoo.

Alternate Transfer Tattoos

Another way of creating a transfer type of tattoo is the same way a real tattoo artist would create a transfer for himself. Using carbon paper over newsprint, draw or copy your design from the carbon paper to the newsprint. Carbon imprint can be transferred from the newsprint to the skin with a little clear deodorant, then the tattoo could be finished, as described above.

Notes:

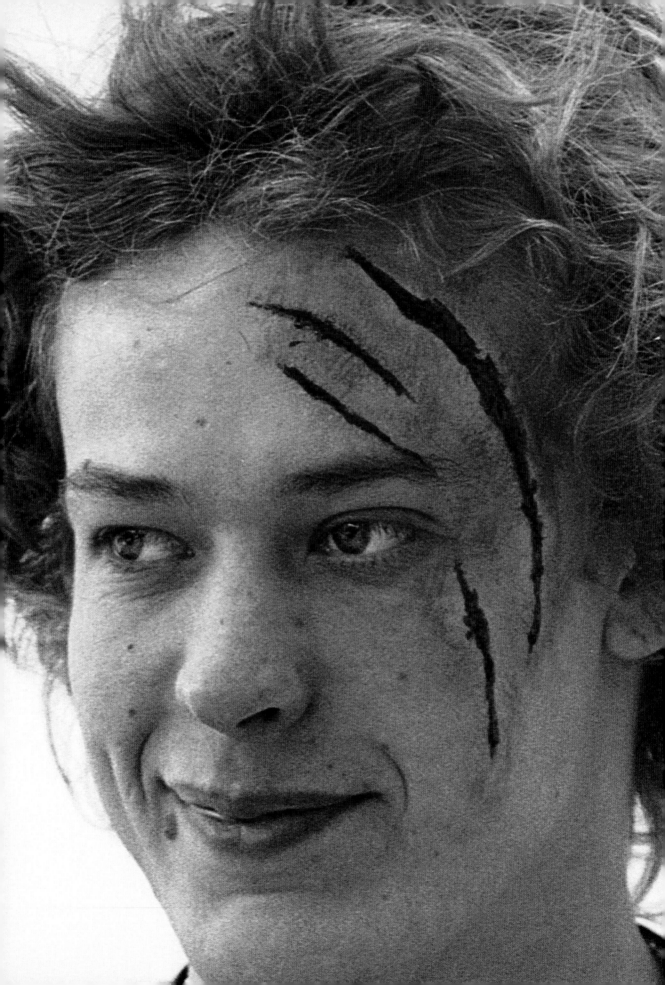

Chapter 14

Injury Simulation

This Chapter is about injuries. We will cover how to use a prosthetic for an injury, and how to create these effects directly on the actor. With unlimited funds a prosthetic can be made for any of these effects, however, often-times on low budget projects, or projects with no preparation time, you will find it necessary to use one of these techniques.

Scars

Scars, of course, are old cuts, so they would follow many of the same principals as cuts. For example, never make them straight, because that would look boring; also they would come in a wide variety of shapes and sizes. There are two types of scars that can be created, indented and raised. Both of these are done almost exactly the same way, with the main material being different in each one. For the indented scar we use Rigid Collodion and for the raised scar we use Tuplast.

The first is the indented scar. Apply Pros-aide to the skin in the desired shape of the scar. Make the adhesive area a little larger than you want the actual scar to be. Do not create an edge with the Pros-aide. Allow the adhesive to dry completely, then apply Rigid Collodion in the shape of the scar directly over the Pros-aide. As the Rigid Collodion dries it will begin to shrink, causing the skin to pucker. Pros-aide is now painted over the entire construction to seal it. Powder the construction to remove the tackiness from the adhesive, using a small amount of K-Y Jelly to remove any powder residue that may remain on the surface of the adhesive. Next, apply color to the construction for the desired effect. Your color choice may be red, maroon, brown, purple, or a light flesh color of rubber mask greasepaint. Before using Rigid Collodion on any performer do a spot test to ensure there is no adverse reaction to the material.

The second is the raised scar or a keloid scar. This is done exactly the same way as the indented scar except, instead of using collodion, a thick plastic material called Tuplast will be used. Apply Pros-aide to the skin in the desired shape of the scar. Make the adhesive area a little larger than you want the actual scar to be.

Allow the adhesive to dry completely, then apply the scar material in the shape of the scar directly over the Pros-aide. Immediately brush the scar material with acetone or 99% alcohol to blend the edges and to give the surface some textural lines through it. Pros-aide is now painted over the entire construction to seal it. Powder the construction to remove the tackiness from the adhesive. Apply a small amount of K-Y Jelly to remove any powder residue that may remain on the surface of the adhesive. Next, apply color to the construction for desired effect. Your color choice may be red, maroon, brown, purple, or a light flesh color of rubber mask grease paint.

Step 1

Apply Pros-aide to the skin in the desired shape of the scar. Make the adhesive area a little larger than you want the actual scar to be. Do not create an edge with the Pros-aide.

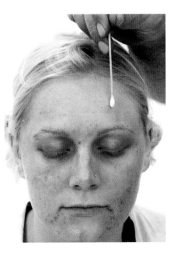

Step 2

Allow the adhesive to dry completely, and then apply Rigid Collodion in the shape of the scar directly over the Pros-aide. As the Rigid Collodion dries it will begin to shrink, causing the skin to pucker.

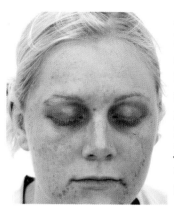

Step 3

Pros-aide is now painted over the entire construction to seal it. Powder the construction to remove the tackiness of the adhesive. Use a small amount of K-Y Jelly to remove any powder residue that may remain on the surface of the adhesive.

Step 4

Next, apply color to the construction for the desired effect. Your color choice may be red, maroon, brown, purple, or a light flesh color of rubber mask grease paint.

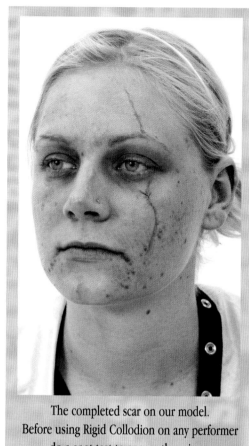

The completed scar on our model. Before using Rigid Collodion on any performer do a spot test to ensure there is no adverse reaction to the material.

Notes:

_____

_____

_____

_____

_____

_____

_____

_____

_____

_____

_____

Wax Cuts

The use of wax in make-up goes back to the days long before prosthetics. In almost every effects project you see, a prosthetic is always used to create a desired effect. So why is it important to learn how to use wax now? Because most projects you see have huge budgets and are well planned. There are, however, lots of low budget projects that can't afford prosthetics. There are also those situations that arise when a director, looking at all the dead people in a room sees one performer and says "wouldn't it be great if". You then have the ability and the know-how to create whatever effect is needed on a moment's notice. The wax you'll be using is a mortician's wax that is typically used in the mortuary business.

Step 1

To create a cut made of wax. Paint spirit gum or Pros-aide onto the area where the injury is to be applied, in the shape you wish, with a cotton swab. Make sure the area of adhesive painted is not too large. It is better to paint the adhesive slightly smaller than the desired area, rather than larger. Make the spirit gum tacky by tapping it with your finger; Pros-aide is tacky when dry. Apply a small amount of cotton over the adhesive, then remove the excess, leaving only a few strands of cotton sticking up out of the adhesive. All that should remain are a few fibers for the wax to adhere to.

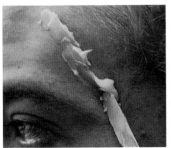

Step 2

Scoop out a small amount of wax with a palette knife and place between your thumb and index finger. Knead the wax until soft, smooth and pliable. Work out any hard spots you may find in the wax.

Step 3

Using the palette knife and small pieces of wax build one side of the cut by applying the wax with a smearing motion to the skin.

Step 4

Next apply wax to the opposite side of the injury in the same fashion as the first side. Keep in mind a straight cut is a boring cut, so keep it interesting by giving your cuts a little shape. Each cut will be unique in design and execution; just as each cut you may receive throughout your life will also be unique.

Step 5

This initial application of wax is considered roughing-out the sculpture only.

Step 6

Starting on one side of the cut, blend the wax downward toward the skin with the palette knife. A light touch is required to give you that subtle blend needed. Repeat on the opposite side.

Step 7

The distance from the top edge of the cut to where it meets the surface of the skin should be, generally, no more than twice the height of the injury.

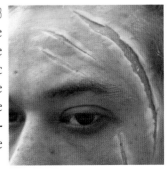

Step 8

The finished sculpture. The wax is now ready to be sealed with latex or plastic sealer. Cut across a white sponge to create a point. The point will allow you to control the application of the latex.

Step 9

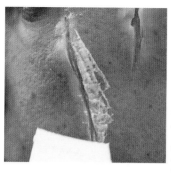

Using the cut wedge sponge stipple a small amount of latex over the entire wax injury. Feather a small amount of latex onto the skin. Dry the latex thoroughly, then powder. Instead of using latex on the construction, you could use plastic sealer. Some artists prefer plastic sealer to latex. (You could try both and formulate your own opinion.)

Step 10

The method of sealing you chose will dictate which type of make-up you can use. If you chose latex, the make-up you would apply is rubber mask grease paint (RMGP). If you chose plastic sealer, you could use regular make-up over the construction. First create a base match by mixing base colors together until you have achieved the perfect match. Apply the color very lightly, as you do not want to over paint a wax construction of this type. Wax, by its very nature, is quite translucent, so only apply enough base to get the wax to match the surrounding skin. Next, apply a red color that will replace that natural redness of the skin into the wax, then powder the make-up very carefully, making sure you do not damage the construction.

Step 11

The next step is to add the bruising which is usually found with this type of injury. Stipple a dark red color (a mixture of Lake Red and #79) over the wax with a brush. This is to simulate the initial bruising that happens when the skin is damaged.

Step 12

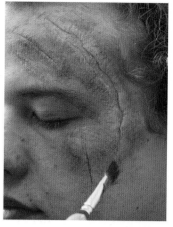

To add shadows to the bruise, apply maroon wherever you may need it.

Step 13

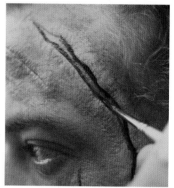

Add black inside the cut to create depth, or you may decide to paint black on the inside edge to create a superficial cut.

Step 14

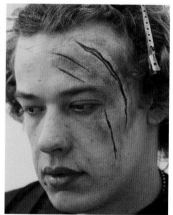

The last thing to do is mix up a small amount of thick and runny blood to create a blood that looks fresh but will also stay where you put it.

Step 15

You can add more blood on set once you know your actor's position and everyone is ready to shoot the effect.

Bullet Wounds: Entrance & Exit

Again we are using wax to create the effect of a bullet entrance and exit wound and, once again, we would use a prosthetic to do this; what is important about this exercise however, is to use large amounts of wax and make it blend in. Up until now we have used as little product as possible to create the effect, but now, through the use of bullet wounds, you will learn how to deal with large amounts of wax.

Before doing our bullet wounds we need to understand what happens when someone is shot. Those that are familiar with a bullet, still may be aware of the fact that the only part of the bullet that leaves the gun is the very tip. This tip moves at an extremely high rate of speed, about 900 feet to 1200 feet per second. When a bullet hits someone it appears the bullet explodes inside of him or her, but that is not the case. What happens is, the bullet enters the body then strikes a bone which is broken from the impact, then the bullet and the bone continue on through the body until they hit something else. This continues until the bullet, and whatever pieces of the person have been ripped out, come shooting out the back. The bullet goes in creating a small hole, but leaving a huge hole as it exits.

The Entrance Wound

To create an entrance wound made of wax, you would apply spirit gum and cotton onto the area where the injury is to be applied, in the same way you would for the cut. Remember, all that should remain are a few fibers of cotton stuck in the spirit gum for the wax to adhere to.

Again, scoop out a small amount of wax with a palette knife placing between your thumb and index finger. Knead the wax until soft, smooth, and pliable, working out any hard spots you may find in it.

The entrance wound is done in the same fashion as the cut. Use the palette knife to apply the wax in a circular shape, leaving the inside edge of the hole sharp and jagged. Blend the outside edge into the skin. This initial application of the wax is considered roughing-out the sculpture only. Blend the wax downward toward the skin with the palette knife. A light touch is required to give you that subtle blend needed. The distance from the top edge of the opening to where it meets the surface of the skin should be, generally, no more than twice the height of the injury.

Using the cut wedge sponge, stipple a small amount of latex over the bullet wound. Dry the latex and then powder it. Also, instead of using latex on the construction you could use plastic sealer.

The method of sealing you chose will dictate which type of make-up you can use. If you chose latex, the make-up you will apply is rubber mask grease paint (RMGP). If you chose plastic sealer, you could use regular make-up over the construction. Because an entrance wound is so small you should only use just enough make-up to cover the wax. First, create a base match by mixing base colors together until you have achieved the perfect match. Apply the color very lightly; you do not want to over-paint a wax construction of this nature. Next, apply a red color that will replace that natural redness of the skin into the wax, then, powder the make-up very carefully, making sure you do not damage the construction. The next step is to add a subtle amount of bruising color to just the edge. Stipple a dark red color over the edge, where the bullet tore the skin, with a brush. This is to simulate the initial bruising that happens when the skin is damaged. Paint black inside the hole to create depth. Finally, mix up a small amount of thick and runny blood to create a blood that looks fresh but will also stay where you put it; more blood can be added once on set.

The Exit Wound

To create the exit wound, we will be applying larger pieces of wax to the skin on the opposite side of the face, creating a ripped open tear that appears to be missing a few chunks of flesh. With the exit wound we are going to use quite a bit of wax to achieve this effect. You want this injury to look deep and very large. We will also add 1/8 inch tubing into our wound to simulate flowing blood.

Large syringes attached to 1/8 inch tubing will be used to propel the blood from the wound. The tubing is made of a soft vinyl, but latex tubing can be used as well.

Step 1

The tubes are glued to the face with Pros-aide adhesive. Apply the glue to both the skin and the tubing, allowing each to completely dry, then press the two together. Placement of the tubes is completely up to you and how you want your wound to bleed.

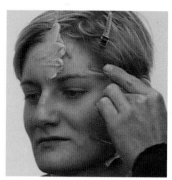

Step 2

Because we are using so much wax you will again use an adhesive and cotton as a base to hold the whole construction in place.

Step 3

The wax will of course blend into the skin, but extra care must be taken to smooth the wax as much as possible with the palette knife. As a final step, you may use a small amount of castor oil or hair gel to help smooth out the wax. Be very careful not to use too much or the oil may cause more problems than it solves.

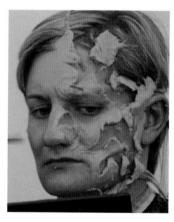

Step 4

The finished application of wax.

Step 5

Using the cut wedge sponge, stipple several layers of latex over the entire wax injury. Feather a small amount of latex onto the skin. Dry the latex thoroughly, then powder.

Step 6

First, create a base match by mixing Rubber Mask Grease Paints together until you have achieved the perfect match. Apply the color all over the wax construction. Wax, by its very nature is quite translucent, but in this case the wax is so thick you have to apply enough base to cover it and then match it to the surrounding skin. You may need to stipple in a few additional base colors to get a good match. Now, apply a red color that will replace that natural redness of the skin into the wax.

Step 7

The next step is to add the bruising to our exit wound. First, powder the make-up very carefully, making sure you do not damage the construction. Stipple a dark red color over the wax along the edge with a brush, then stipple more dark red around to color the wax and to create an interesting bruise. To add shadows to the exit wound apply maroon wherever you may need it.

Step 8

Add black inside the various cuts that make up our exit wound to create depth. Put the black only in the deepest areas. The other areas can be painted maroon or a dark red color.

Step 9

The last thing to do is add our mixture of thick and runny blood to the inside of the injury. This will help to keep the inside of our wound fresh looking. The hair is used to disguise the tubes running to the wound.

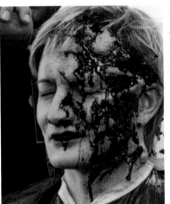

Step 10

Adding thinned blood to each syringe. Hold the syringe above the injury to allow the blood to flow into the tubing. Then lower the syringe to stop the blood from leaking out into the wound.

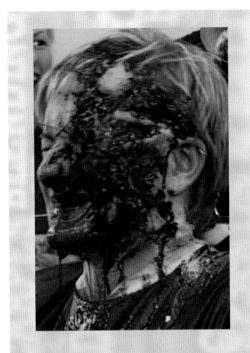

The final effect of the blood oozing from the wound. By squeezing all four syringes at the same time, the blood appears to be flowing from all over inside the wound.

Notes:

Prosthetic Injury

Prosthetics are the best choice for most injuries because every piece looks the same. As a matter of fact, they are made from the same mold and are exactly the same each day they have to be applied. It is essential in most situations that your make-up matches exactly from day to day. For the following prosthetic make-up we are using a foam gelatin prosthetic. However, an injury prosthetic could be made out of any of the other prosthetic materials referred to in prior chapters.

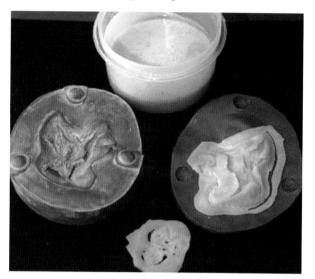

The foam gelatin prosthetic right after it has been de molded. We are using an appliance to simulate a gun shot wound through the cheek. The lower appliances are the entrance wound and the appliance on the mold is the exit wound. Before we start, all of the mold release needs to be removed or washed off the gelatin appliances. Using 99% alcohol and a brush, gently scrub the prosthetic appliances clean. The mold release can cause your prosthetic appliances to not stick to the skin very well.

Step 1
The back of the prosthetic appliance needs to be sealed before it is applied. We use a combination of Pros-aide adhesive and Fixer Spray. Apply three layers of each, alternating each layer. The Pros-aide is applied first and then the Fixer Spray. Apply this combination three times.

Step 2
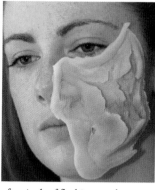

Once the prosthetic has been thoroughly sealed it can be applied to the skin. To attach to the skin apply Pros-aide adhesive to the skin and to the back of the prosthetic. Put two matching spots on the skin and the prosthetic, allowing both to dry, then press them together. Leave about a quarter of an inch of flashing on the prosthetic, this will help keep the edges straight.

Step 3

Apply adhesive to the skin under the appliance, work out to the edges and allow to dry, then press the appliance into the glue. Work all around the prosthetic in this fashion until the edges are secure. Next, use a small amount of Witch Hazel to dissolve and separate the flashing from the rest of the prosthetic. Be very careful with the Witch Hazel as a little goes a long way.

Step 4

With the prosthetic completely applied, use Pros-aide and Fixer Spray over the entire appliance to seal it. This is done in the same way as the inside was sealed. Pros-aide is applied first and allowed to dry, then the Fixer Spray is applied over the adhesive. All of the Pros-aide must be covered with Fixer Spray before moving on to color.

Step 5
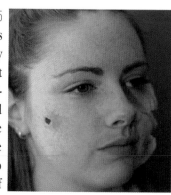

The entrance wound in this make-up was done exactly the same as the larger exit wound. Once both appliances are applied and properly blended, you are now ready to color. Since the prosthetics are so translucent, thin washes of make-up are applied over them helping them blend with the surrounding skin color.

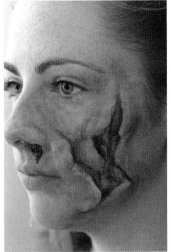

Step 6

Shadows and highlights can be applied with the same type of make-up as the base color. The bruising colors should also be applied at this point. Make sure you powder between the base colors and the red bruising colors, ensure that the bruising colors do not become pink. Apply the reds and maroons along the opening of the cut, then apply the bruising into the shadows to help further blend the prosthetic.

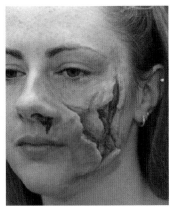

Step 7

Line the opening of the wound with black and add a little visual interest inside the wound. Red can be painted on the inside to simulate the muscle color and white can be used for the fat and bone.

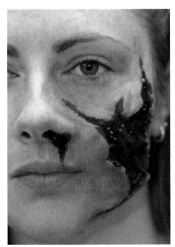

Step 8

Thick and regular blood are mixed together to create a gel blood that has chunks in it. It also helps the blood to stick inside the wound. You can add blood running from the wound once you are on set and the performer is placed.

Notes:

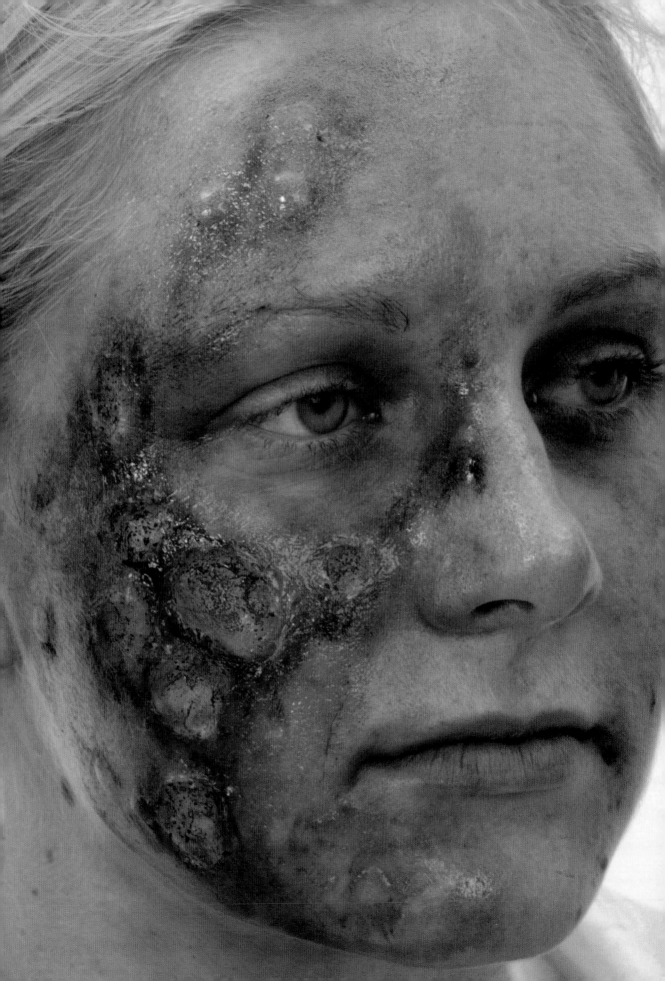

Chapter 15

Burns

Many things can cause burns, the most common being fire, but chemicals, water, steam, the sun, and just about anything hot can also cause them.

There are three classifications of burns, namely 1st degree, 2nd degree, and 3rd degree. 1st degree is the least severe, while 3rd degree is the severist. The most common example of a 1st degree burn is sunburn. The characteristics of a 1st degree burn are redness and shine. A 2nd degree burn also has the same redness as a 1st, but is accompanied by blisters. A third degree burn is the complete and total destruction of skin, and is usually surrounded by first and second degree burns; except when caused by something as hot as a branding iron.

When creating these burns, it is advisable to have plenty of reference material to view and copy. Proper research is essential in the reproduction of any injury.

1st Degree Burn

Begin with a white sponge and a red color. Cut the edges off the white sponge to minimize streaks in your make-up, applying redness with the white sponge in an even pattern. The redder the color, the more severe the burn will appear. When applying to the face for the effect of sunburn, apply the make-up to the high points in the face such as the cheekbones, forehead, and the top of the nose, then apply a layer of K-Y Jelly over the red areas, to give them the necessary shine.

2nd Degree Burn

This burn is done somewhat differently, even though it is the same as a 1st degree with the addition of blisters. First, apply Tuplast to the skin in the shape of a bubble being aware that, not all blisters are the same size and shape; make sure you vary the size and shape of each blister. Also, keep in mind that the placement of each blister should be random and not evenly spaced. Secondly, place latex over the blisters with a white sponge. Apply at least three layers making sure you dry each layer with a hair dryer before proceeding to the next layer.

Using a pair of tweezers, tear open the latex that is covering some of the Tuplast. The Tuplast will also rip open and the hole will look like a popped blister. Because this construction is made up of latex we must use a RMGP. Choose a bright red color, such as Kryolan's #79, and mix it with a small amount of 99% alcohol; apply as a wash over the latex construction. Since the latex and Tuplast are translucent there is no reason to use a flesh color or to heavily cover the construction in make-up. Once a nice red stain is achieved apply maroon RMGP half way around each blister, alternating the sides of the blister that get the color. This will give the illusion of soreness and depth. Lightly apply a small amount of red RMGP into the open blisters. Castor oil mixed with a yellow green color can be applied to the open blisters to simulate pus.

3rd Degree Burn

The third degree burn is the worst of all burns. To properly create this effect – you must first build up layers of skin then tear the layers of skin off to simulate the skin that has been burnt away.

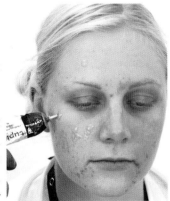

Step 1

Start this burn the same way as the 2nd degree burn by applying Tuplast in spots wherever you need the 3rd degree to be, then apply more Tuplast around that first area in the shape of the blisters you want around your 3rd degree burn. Remember not all blisters are the same size and shape, so make sure you vary the size and shape of each blister. Also keep in mind the placement of each blister should be random and not evenly spaced.

Step 2

Next apply latex over all of the Tuplast with a white sponge. Apply at least three layers and make sure you dry each layer with a hair dryer before proceeding to the next layer.

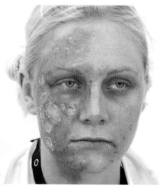

Step 3

Once all the latex is dry, tear holes in it, tearing off all the Tuplast that is in the 3rd degree burn area. (The holes in the latex should be of varying sizes and shapes.) Using a pair of tweezers, tear open the latex that is covering some of the Tuplast in the blister area; the Tuplast will also tear open and the hole will look like a popped blister.

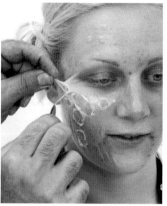

Step 4

Just like the 2nd degree burn the construction is made up of latex, which means RMGP must be used. Choose a bright red color such as Kryolan's #79 and mix it with a small amount of 99% alcohol. Apply as a wash over the entire latex construction. Again, the latex and Tuplast are translucent so there is no reason to use a flesh color or to heavily cover the construction in make-up.

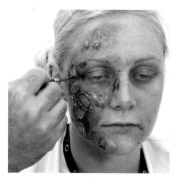

Step 5

Once a nice red stain is achieved over the entire construction, simulating the 1st degree burn, apply maroon RMGP half way around each blister and on the inside edge of each hole. This will give the illusion of soreness and depth to each blister and to each hole. Lightly apply a small amount of red RMGP into the open blisters.

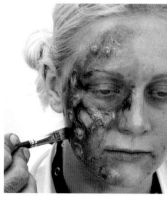

Step 6

Next, apply black RMGP around each hole and blend out onto the surrounding area. The black simulates charring caused by fire, however if this is a chemical burn there will be no black.

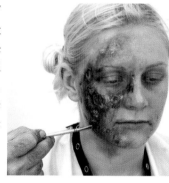

Step 7

The final touch is the light application of blood inside the holes. Allow the blood to bead up on the surface, creating the look of the blood seeping from the burned away areas.

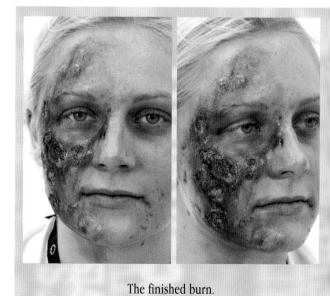

The finished burn.

3rd Degree Burn Variation

This version of a 3rd degree burn is a more exaggerated version of the first. Apply spirit gum to the skin in the shape of the burn to be created, and, with a finger, tap the adhesive until it becomes tacky. Press the cotton into adhesive then remove the excess cotton, leaving only small fibers sticking up from the adhesive. Mix a small amount of gelatin with a heated mixture of glycerin and sorbitol. Stir in the gelatin until a creamy consistency is achieved, then add a drop or two of liquid blood for an appropriate color. With a palette knife, spread the gelatin over the edges of the cotton, creating a thin edge. Take the remainder of the gelatin mixture and apply to the center of the cotton area. Cover all exposed cotton with gelatin mixture. Using a palette knife, manipulate the gelatin and the cotton to look like muscle tissue. Allow the gelatin mixture to dry thoroughly. Apply Tuplast to the skin around the gelatin, in the shape of a bubble. Remember, not all blisters are the same size and shape, so make sure you vary the size and shape of each one. Also, keep in mind the placement of each blister should be random and not evenly spaced. Next, apply latex over the blisters and the gelatin with a white sponge. Apply at least three layers, making sure you dry each layer with a hair dryer before proceeding to the next layer. Once all the latex is dry,

tear holes in the latex, revealing the gelatin beneath. (The holes in the latex should be of varying sizes and shapes.) Again, using a pair of tweezers, tear open the latex that is covering some of the Tuplast in the blister area. The Tuplast will also rip open and the hole will look like a popped blister. Just like the 2nd degree burn the construction is made up of latex, which means RMGP must be used. This time, however, a flesh tone RMGP must be used to create a realistic skin color. Now choose a bright red color, such as Kryolan's #79, and mix it with a small amount of 99% alcohol; apply as a wash over the entire latex construction. Once a nice red stain is achieved over the entire construction, simulating the 1st degree burn, apply maroon RMGP half way around each blister. But this time not only will we apply maroon on the inside edge of each hole but also into each nook and crevice. This will give the illusion of soreness and depth to each blister and to each hole. Lightly apply a small amount of red RMGP into the open blisters and apply black RMGP around each hole, blending out onto the surrounding area. The black simulates charring caused by fire, however if this is a chemical burn then there will be no black. The final touch is the light application of blood inside the holes.

Notes:

_____

_____

_____

_____

_____

_____

_____

_____

_____

_____

_____

_____

_____

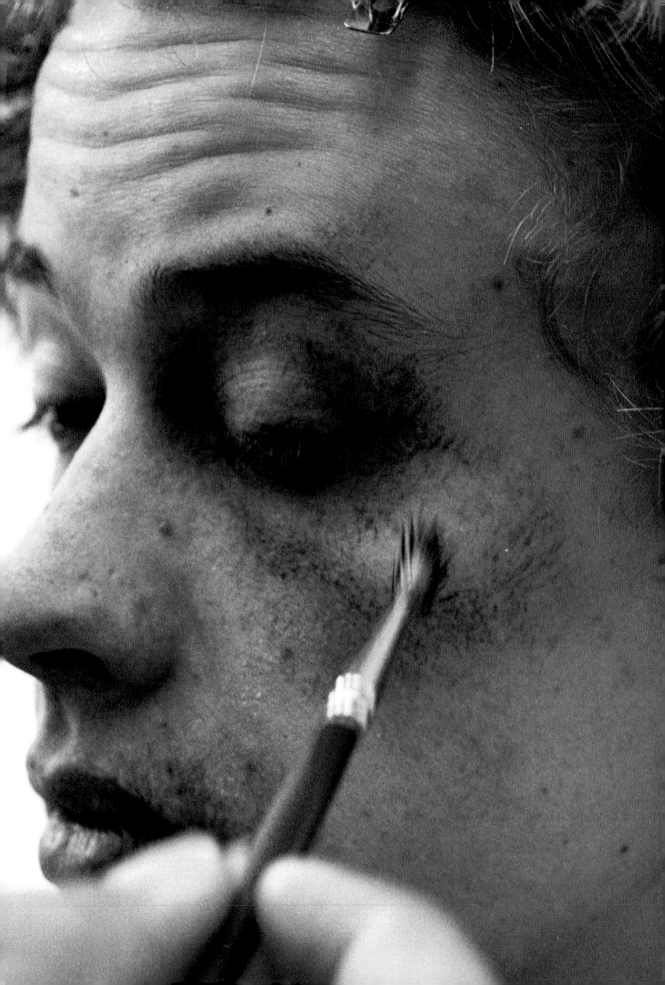

Chapter 16

Character Effects

This chapter deals with all those simple small effects that come up as you are working. Usually these can be achieved a variety of ways and we will explore all the possibilities.

Tears

A typical effect that can happen in the most effect free film is crying. Yes, this is an effect. Some actors have the ability to cry on demand, while others may need a moment to think of something really sad. Quite often the make-up artist is required to fill in when actors can't make themselves cry. There are a couple of ways to accomplish this, one being the use of a menthol blower. The blower is a glass tube with a cap on each side. Menthol crystals are placed inside between two pieces of cotton; and then wrap the front of the blower with a piece of panty hose. The panty hose will ensure that the crystals wil not accidentally be blown into the actor's eye. Then you simply aim one end of the tube towards the actor's eye and blow (gently, of course, as the menthol irritates the eye, causing it to tear). When you need actors to look like they have been crying for hours, redden around the nose and eyes, using glycerin to drip down their cheeks. Keep the glycerin out of the actor's eyes.

Sweat

To get the look of perspiration use a mixture of water and glycerin, applying it with a sponge to the areas you want to be shiny. Glycerin will bead up on the skin so if you need additional beading use more glycerin than water. Since the glycerin is so thick it is easy to maintain continuity. For fight scenes, where the director wants to do the slow motion punch and the actor receiving the punch whips his head around, causing droplets of sweat to fly off of him, use water only. Right before you shoot, simply spray the actor down with water and the slow motion camera will pick up every drop.

Dirt

When discussing any kind of dirt we need to talk about all kinds of dirt, including, but not limited to grease, oil, mud, dust, grime, ash, soot, etc. First of all, determine what material you will use. Cosmetic manufacturers have a variety of products to help simulate many of these effects, however sometimes it is best to simply use the real thing. Light and dark powders are great for dirt and dust, whereas eyeshadow can be used in some situations. The best solution is to test your ideas prior to the shoot, trying different combinations.

Ice & Snow Effects

Ice and snow are the easy part of this make-up. What we are really creating is a look of severe exposure. Whether you choose a burn look or a freezing look will affect which color you will choose. For this exposure make-up we used more reds to simulate soreness to the skin as well as a pale tone to simulate the lack of blood circulation.

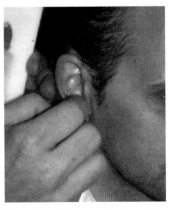

Step 1

First start with a quick 1st degree burn to the face simulating windburn. Begin with a white sponge and a red color. Cut the edges off the white sponge to minimize streaks in your make-up; the redder the color, the more severe the burn will appear. When applying to the face for the effect of windburn, apply the make-up to the high points in the face such as the cheekbones, forehead, and the top of the nose.

Step 2

An orange sponge can also be used to apply your colors to the face. The nice thing about the orange sponge is the texture it will create on the skin. You can stipple on both the red and the pale base.

Step 3

Apply the pale base over the high areas of the face. This will help sink in the eyes a little and start to show the skin in an unhealthy condition. Add a little blue to the eyelid area and the lips. Now you are ready to apply the Ultra Ice.

Step 4

Ultra Ice is a gel material that simulates ice on the skin. Using a pallet knife apply the gel in the hair, to the tip of the nose, eyebrows, and ears. You can even create icicles by applying it heavy and allowing it to remain sharp in parts.

Step 5

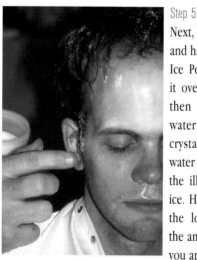

Next, lightly spritz the face and hair with water. Apply Ice Powder by sprinkling it over the face and hair then spritz with more water. The Ice Powder crystals will absorb the water and swell creating the illusion of snow and ice. How severe you want the look will determine the amount of Ice Powder you apply.

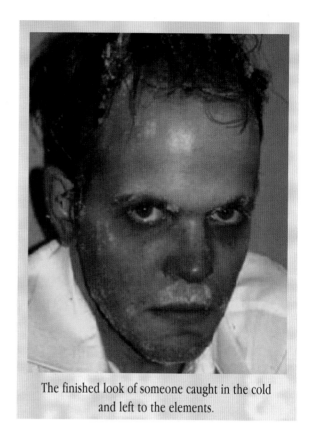

The finished look of someone caught in the cold and left to the elements.

Blood Formula

There are as many blood formulas as there are make-up artists, with most of them creating a believable effect. However, when a film requires a bleeding effect it is usually advisable to purchase blood from a manufacturer of blood. There are three reasons to buy blood rather than make your own. First, I like the color of the blood that most manufacturers are creating. The thickness and translucency of the blood available is getting quite good. Secondary, the cost of buying pre-made blood is about the same as driving around and picking up the ingredients, plus the time involved in mixing it up in the kitchen. When you look at all those cost factors and your time and effort, you realize that it is more cost effective to purchase it pre-done. Finally, and maybe most importantly, if an actor has an adverse reaction to the blood the liability rests solely on the shoulders of the manufacturer. As long as you are using the blood within the guidelines the manufacturer sets out then you are relatively protected.

But, if you are going to force me to give you a formula then here it is. A classic formula used by many artist starting out and which they have subsequently expanded upon and developed to suit their individual needs is:

Start with half a gallon of Karo syrup, add red food coloring to a good clear bright red, then add 2 drops of green and one drop of blue to give your blood that dark undertone. Cornstarch is used to give the proper thickness; this should be added slowly until you reach the right thickness for you.

Blood Knife

We are referring to a gag that makes it appear as if you are cutting someone with a real knife.

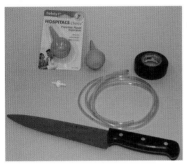

Step 1

The materials required to create the blood knife effect. Ball syringe, 1/8 inch inside diameter tubing, tubing connector, black electrical tape, and a real knife.

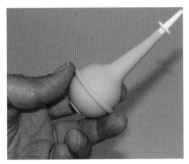

Step 2

Slip the connector into the ball syringe.

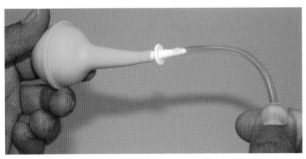

Step 3

Attach the tubing to the connector. The ball syringe is attached only to help with the placement.

Step 4

The knife we are using is a real knife, so before we use it we need to dull it. A dremel moto tool is used to flatten the edge. Anything that will grind down metal will work.

Step 5

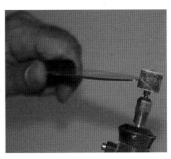

Make sure every part of the blade is dull before using it. You do not want to accidently cut an actor with a knife that has not been dulled down properly.

Step 6

Using black electrical tape, attach the connector and the ball syringe to the handle. Make sure you know which side will be to camera.

Step 7

Next tape the tubing into position. Run it close to the cutting edge of the blade.

Step 8

Cut the tubing to length. We cut the tube at an angle so the end is a little easier to hide.

Step 9

Tape the end closed with the electrical tape.

Step 10

Then tape the end of the tube down to the knife, again making sure the

tube is close to the cutting edge of the knife.

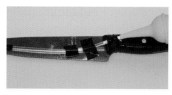

Step 11

Cut away the tape holding the ball syringe. Re-tape the connector to ensure it is not going to move.

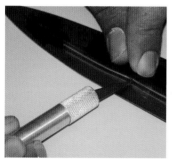

Step 12

The ball syringe is removable, allowing easy filling.

Step 13

One more piece of tape is applied along the back of the tubing to ensure it does not move when blood is pumped through it.

Step 14

Use an X-acto knife to cut small slits into the bottom of the tube. The blood will flow from these small slits.

Step 15

Pour blood into a separate container. You may need to add water to it to thin it. The blood may be too thick to flow easily through the tubing.

Step 16

Squeeze the ball syringe and insert into the blood. As you release the pressure on the syringe the blood will be sucked up into the syringe.

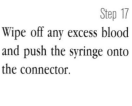

Step 17

Wipe off any excess blood and push the syringe onto the connector.

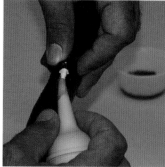

Step 18

The finished knife, ready to be used.

Step 19

As you squeeze the syringe the blood oozes out of the slits in the tube.

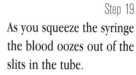

Step 20

When you are ready to do the effect on camera. Instruct the actor on how to use the knife. Place the blade to the skin and as you drag the knife across the skin squeeze the syringe.

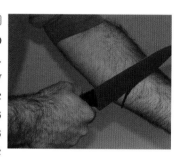

The knife will create a nice straight line of blood, giving the illusion you are really cutting into the skin.

As you can see this needs to be a quick type of an effect, for if the camera lingers on the cut it will spoil the effect.

Bladders

Bladders are small latex pockets used to create an on-camera swelling effect. They are applied under a prosthetic appliance and inflated with air to make it appear as if the skin is swelling. This can be used for a multitude of effects. The way we make bladders can also be used to create flat tubing, such as for the exit wound. The following is a step-by-step process for a bladder or for a flat tube.

Step 1

First, draw your design for the bladder on a piece of white paper, then cut out the shape, making a template. Trace your template onto a piece of black plastic, such as a black trash bag. The template allows you to repeat your drawing over and over. Again, you can make the bladder any shape you want.

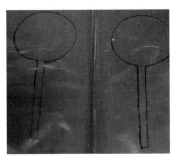

Step 2

In this demonstration we are using the same size bladder over and over, but you could trace a variety of shapes and sizes, with no limit to the possibilities.

Step 3

Any smooth surface will work to build the bladder. Here we are using a smooth piece of wood that has wax applied to it and then buffed smooth.

Step 4

Lay your cut out pieces of plastic on the board and draw a line around the plastic about a quarter of an inch from the plastic. This will allow for sturdy edges around the bladder.

Step 5

Remove the plastic and stipple latex onto the board over your drawn on bladders. Four layers will be needed. Stipple the first layer onto the board, then allow to dry half way, until about medium rare. Stipple a second layer over the first before the first layer is completely dry. Apply each of the four layers in the same fashion. The layers of latex will bond to each other better if they are only half dry. Be careful not to damage the previous layer with the application of the subsequent layer.

Step 6

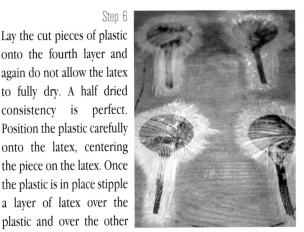

Lay the cut pieces of plastic onto the fourth layer and again do not allow the latex to fully dry. A half dried consistency is perfect. Position the plastic carefully onto the latex, centering the piece on the latex. Once the plastic is in place stipple a layer of latex over the plastic and over the other layers of latex. Apply the latex in the same fashion as before, again applying four layers of latex on top of the plastic.

Step 7

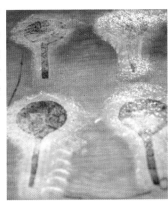

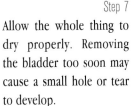

Allow the whole thing to dry properly. Removing the bladder too soon may cause a small hole or tear to develop.

Step 8
Powder the entire bladder with powder; un-powdered latex will stick to itself.

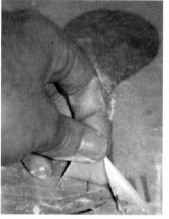

Step 9
Carefully lift the edge of the bladder up and powder on the bottom side of the piece. Peel the whole piece off the board.

Step 10
Once the bladder is removed, powder it and trim off the excess edge.

Step 11
Cut the end off the bladder's long tail, exposing the plastic. Fill a ball syringe with powder and force air and powder into the bladder. The powder will coat the interior of the bladder and keep it from sticking to itself. Once you are sure there is a sufficient amount of powder inside the bladder use a pair of tweezers to pull the plastic out. You may choose to leave the plastic in if you are planning to only inflate the bladder with air. However, if you want fluid to flow through the bladder then you will need to remove the plastic; the bladder is now ready to be applied under a prosthetic.

Applying Bladders

For a bladder to work properly you must ensure it has enough room to expand. Only apply adhesive to the center bottom, the part of the bladder that touches the skin. Also, only apply the prosthetic around the bladder. No glue should be on top of the bladder; the adhesive used to adhere the prosthetic should go around the bladder.

Chapter 17

Working as a Make-up Artist

For a make-up artist, understanding how this business works is as important as knowing how to apply eyeshadow. This chapter will cover those aspects of the make-up profession often overlooked.

Attitude

Your attitude is the single most important tool you possess. Your attitude will take you places your talent will never be able to reach. Film making is an art form that is a collaboration of many talents and the truth is production would rather hire a person with a good attitude and personality than the most talented artist. When we say good attitude what do we mean? The first is a positive attitude, always in a good mood and smiling, willing to help in every way possible, anticipating the actors' and production's needs at all times. Now, all this niceness may make a few of you nauseous, but what we are saying is, when you work on set always realize your next job can come from anywhere and anyone there. So be respectful of every person, whether it be the director or an extra.

Continuity

One of the more important aspects of our job is to maintain continuity of the make-up. Films take a long time to make and some scenes can take several days to film, sometimes only representing a few minutes of screen time in which our actor is all within the same time frame of the story. Our job is to ensure we are using the same colors on the actors every day, making sure when the scene is cut together there are no changes in the make-up.

There are many ways artists maintain continuity, one being with a polaroid camera. (Take a picture, writing the scene number on the bottom.) Another way to do it is to write good notes about how each make-up is done in every scene; some projects may require both techniques. The one problem with a Polaroid print is the picture quality is not that good, making it difficult to see detail and color.

Face Charts

A face chart is a tool used by artist to design make-ups and to convey those designs to other artists or production. They are not used to convey an idea but to show how an idea will lay out on the face. The face chart can also be used for continuity purposes; by outlining the make-up on a face chart an artist will know what color to use and where to place it. These are especially helpful when doing pick up shots.

Test Shoots

Often an under-used tool in a production's bag of tricks. Whenever you are starting a project that requires a character make-up outside the norm of beauty make-up, request a test shoot. A test shoot is prior to the first day of shooting. The camera is rented and film is purchased; you do the make-up you are planning and then, a day later the film is processed, giving you the opportunity of viewing the character on screen, analyzing the effect and making any necessary adjustments based on what you see. This will also give production a clear understanding of what to expect on the first day of shooting and what they will see on film.

Script Breakdown

The first step in film production no matter what you are doing on the film. As the key make-up artist your job is to first read the script and then take notes on it. You never want to be that person on set asking what is going on. You want to know what is happening all the time. The single best way to do this is to read the script and understand it completely, I recommend reading it twice. The first time would be to read it in order to understand the story, and the second time to highlight all the characters and the different make-ups.

In the script you may read "Bob enters the room meeting Teri for the first time". Since this is the first time we are meeting Teri in the script, her name or the line on which it appears, should be highlighted. By the same token if the script says "Teri turns and punches Bob in the nose" (I will highlight this line so I know there is a make-up there.) Once all the make-up aspects of the project have been highlighted, the scene numbers, who is in the scene and what their make-up is in that scene, should be written down. If you have any questions for production about a character such as: "Do you want Bob's nose to bleed?" write it down, with the scene number, on a separate piece of paper. This is also the beginning of keeping accurate records and doing a good job with continuity.

Research

As an artist, research is essential to you in creating the best look and effect. Whether you are doing a realistic aging make-up or the current trends in eye shadow, it is nice to start off with some sort of basic idea of what you could do; research is a term we use to describe the process of looking at reality and then building those elements into our make-up. It does not matter if you are looking at other artists creations or at real life. Research can be the source of inspiration for a character, by combining elements we see in the everyday world and adding them to your character.

Set Etiquette

The subject of etiquette can also be called professionalism. Attitude is everything on a set; once again, you never know where your next job is coming from, so be respectful of everyone. Working on films is a long process and often you will be sitting around doing nothing.

Touch Ups

When learning make-up it is hard to understand what a touch up is until you are actually doing make-up on a project. It is your responsibility to make sure your character's make-up, whether it is a beauty make-up or an elaborate prosthetic make-up, looks the same as when you applied it. This is the essence of touching up make-up. You should not rush in between every take to powder your actor. Rather, you should only touch him/her up when you see a problem that needs to be corrected. Your job as a make-up artist is to be close to the camera, keeping an eye on your make-up. If you see unwanted shine then you can go in, but only when you see a problem.

Doing the touch up is very similar to doing the make-up in the first place. You should have the colors, materials, and tools you used. Also you should be thinking about what might happen on set that may be necessary to fix. A common mistake is to simply powder everyone as a way of touching them up. You really should only powder a few times a day. In most cases a tissue wrapped around a powder puff can be used to absorb excess oil. If you keep powdering the actor over and over you will end up with mud.

The Make-up Kit

Your make-up kit is your tool box. There is a list of tools in chapter one, which will give you an idea of the utensils you will need to work as a make-up artist. These tools, of course, should be in

your kit. In addition to these tools is all the make-up you may need to complete a particular project. The following is a list of all the additional things you may need in your kit. You may not carry everything with you all the time but rather separate into smaller bags or kits that can be brought for specific projects. As a make-up artist you should try to be prepared for any eventuality. This is not always possible, but we do try. This list gives you an idea of what you may need. It also includes items you may want to have with you on a project, which are usually moved into a trailer instead of being carried with you all the time.

Additional Items for your Kit

Cell Phone	Business Cards
Application Notes	Utility Bag
Rubber Bands	Pencil Sharpener
Sewing Kit	Shaving Cream
Zip Lock Bags	Wash Cloths
Ever Blum (cosmetic stain remover)	35mm or Digital Camera
Moisturizer	Super Matte Anti-shine
Make-up Remover Towelettes	Small On-Set Chair
Swiss Army Knife or Small tool Kit	Eye Dropper
Mints	Gum
Toothbrush	Tooth Paste
Mouth Wash	Hand Held Mirror
Straws	Make-up Chair
Breath Spray	Oil Absorbing Spray
Non-latex Make-up Sponge	Sharpie Marker
Mascara	Concealers
Empty Container for Brush Cleaner	Small Plastic Cups
Eye Lash Curler	Double Sided Tape
Scotch Tape	Safety Pins
Visine	Krazy Glue
Emery Board	Cotton Balls
Nail Polish Remover	Nail Clippers
Glycerin (sweat)	Extra Spray Bottles
Sea Sponge	Blood Capsules
Small container to stand up pencils and brushes	

Hair Supplies

Hair Scrunchies	Head Bands
Bobby Pins	Hair Pins
Hair Spray	Matrix Quick Dry Spray
Hayshi Spray Shine	Thermal Set Mist
Curl Relax Balm	Styling Glaze

Spray Gel	Mousse
Hot Rollers	Roller Clamps
Clips	Wave Clamps
Marcelle Grip Curling Irons	Hair Dryer
Hair Ribbons	Hair Bands
Coated Ponytail Holders	Squeeze Type Hair Clips
Extension Cord	Plug Adapter
Tint Brush	Streaks & Tips
Hair white	Wig Cap
Wahl Clippers	
Brushes - Round, Vented, Thermal, and Styling	
Combs - Wide Tooth, Rattail, Styling Hair Pick	

Personal Items For Location Shooting

Hip Pack	Water
Vitamins	Personal Bag (Back Pack)
Pillow	Bathroom Supplies

Desert / Hot Location

Sunscreen	Hat
Small Cooler for on Set Make-up	Sunglasses
Bandana (to wet around neck)	Umbrella
Mister or Spray Bottle with Fan	Aloe Vera Gel

First Aid Kit

First Aid Kit	Bar of Soap
Feminine Hygiene Products	Aspirin & Tylenol
Dental Floss	Throat lozenges
Cold Remedies	

The Different Mediums

We could write a complete book for every medium and how each make-up relates to it. Instead, we thought we would shed some light on these subjects and talk about their individual properties. Some artists work only in one of these mediums, whereas, other artists may work in many mediums. When asked how to paint a prosthetic appliance, the question "in which medium?" should always arise before that question can be answered; depending on the way we are viewing that prosthetic appliance may require different ways of coloring it. The way we shoot things has changed so drastically over the past few years, there is no pat answer for any make-up technique.

Film

Film, when viewed, is a very large image and can be most critical. What this means for us is, for example, if we do eyeliner that is too thick on a film then, when it is projected on the screen, that same eyeliner may be six inches in thickness. Typically we shoot on 35mm and 70mm film, and as each frame is exposed to light it burns those colors onto the negative. The colors we choose for film projects tend to stay more true. With film production it is "what you see is what you get". That means, a very natural make-up should be applied, not a heavy or obvious application. Where film is viewed will also affect your decisions on which make-up techniques should be used. If you are working on a feature film, to be shown in the local theater, then your make-up should be thin and natural. If you are filming a television show, you have more options in terms of the types of make-ups you do.

Television and Video

Television refers to the way some projects are viewed, not how they are shot. Remember, when working on a project planned for either direct-to-video or specifically, a television show, that the image on a television set is usually smaller than life-size. This means, you can get away with using more make-up. When working in video you have a new set of circumstances to deal with. Video is an electronic interpretation of an image. The camera shoots 30 frames of video per second, with each frame consisting of a series of dots and every dot being assigned a color. Video also has a lower range of color than film, so some of the colors you are using on your actor may change. You may apply a red orange lip color to an actress and find when you view her on the monitor that her lip color has changed slightly. Therefore, finding the right colors to use in a video project is a challenge. When working on a project being shot on video you will have to take a look at the monitor in the technical director's booth. That monitor will be the most accurate.

Digital

Digital is the newest of the mediums. Digital filming is now catching on as 24 perf cameras are developed. This type of process is very similar to film. The colors are excellent, the image quality being the same as film. The differences are not so apparent in the filming process as in the projection of the film. It is almost impossible to tell the difference between a film shot on digital or one shot on film, when it is projected normally, but when you see a film projected digitally it is a little brighter. What does this mean for make-up artists? It means our make-ups need to be even more subtle. We should strive for imperceptible make-up.

Print

Probably the most critical of all mediums simply because it is a non-moving frame of film. Print includes both digital prints and film prints and both may require different approaches. Photographs can sometimes be larger than life, which will also further exploit any imperfection in the make-up. The viewer also has the opportunity to study a photograph closely. The use of an airbrush on photographs was developed to help create flawless women.

Stage

Theater is the most forgiving of all the mediums. That is not to say theater make-up is easy, just that the audience is further away than any other viewing audience. The make-up you do for a stage production will be more intense. The techniques for applying the make-up are the same as any other medium. Depending on how big the house is will depend how intense you go. In some intimate house of only a hundred seats you will find you are doing the same type of make-up as you are for film.

Notes:

GLOSSARY OF TERMS

A

99% Alcohol: Colorless volatile inflammable liquid used to thin make-up.

Accentuate: To emphasize or to make prominent.

Acetone: Colorless volatile liquid that dissolves organic compounds.

Acrylic Paint: Water based paint that is commonly used by artist and mixed with Pros-aide to make Pax Paint.

Adhesive: A sticky material used to attach items together.

Adverse: Unfavorable or harmful reaction.

Age Spots: A discoloration on the surface of the skin caused by the aging process.

Age Stipple: The process of using latex to create wrinkles in the skin.

Aging: The process of growing old.

Airbrush: A small hand held spray gun used for spraying paint or make-up onto a subject.

Allergy: An adverse reaction to certain substances.

Application: The technique used to put a make-up product on the model.

Anchoring Point: A strong spot of adhesive used to hold a bald cap or prosthetic appliance in place.

B

Bald: Lacking some or all hair on the scalp.

Bald Cap: The name of the appliance used to create the effect of a bald person.

Bald Cap Form: A form used to make a bald cap.

Base Color: A flesh tone make-up.

Base Match: A flesh tone make-up that matches the performer perfectly.

Beard: Facial hair.

Black Stipple Sponge: A type of sponge with a large cell structure used to create scrapes and beard stubble.

Blister: A small bubble on the skin filled with fluid and caused by heat or friction.

Blood: Red fluid circulating in the arteries and veins of humans.

Bondo: Cab-o-sil and Pros-aide mixed together to a creamy paste used to fill in depressions.

Brick Color: A red color used as an undertone on prosthetics. Also used to add subtle redness to a face.

Brittle: Hard and fragile, apt to break easily.

Brow bone: The protrusion of bone that the eyebrow rests upon. In eyeshadow treatments, highlight is placed under the eyebrow and along the base of the brow bone.

Bruise: Injury and discoloration of the skin.

Bullet: a small pointed missile fired from a gun.

Bullet Wound: Injury to the skin caused by sudden impact with a bullet.

Burn: Injury caused by fire or chemicals.

C

Cab-o-sil: Fumed silica used to make chemicals thicker.

Canister: A container of compressed gas.

Capillaries: A branching blood vessel connecting arteries and veins.

Carbon Dioxide: A non-flammable gas, used as an airbrush propellant.

Casting Urethane: A rigid water-soluble crystalline compound.

Castor Oil: Oil from the seeds of a tropical plant, used as a purgative and lubricant.

Cheekbone: Bone below the eye, also known as the Zygomatic arch.

Cheek Color: A make-up product that is applied to the center of the cheekbone. It can either be a cream or powdered product.

Clavicle: Collarbone.

Clay: A stiff sticky earth used to sculpt prosthetics.

Coagulate: When blood changes from a liquid to a semisolid or clot.

Colored Pencils: Artist pencils in a variety of colors.

Compressor: A machine used for compressing air for use with an airbrush.

Concoction: A mixture of ingredients.

Construction: The process of building a character on the actor's face.

Contour: The process of highlight and shading that achieves a desired effect.

Corners of the Mouth: Where the upper and lower lips meet.

Cotton: A soft white fibrous substance.

Cotton Swabs: A soft white fibrous substance on a stick.

Coverage: A term used to describe how translucent or how opaque a make-up is.

Crease: A deep line or wrinkle in the face.

Crepe Wool: Wool fibers used to simulate hair.

Crown: This refers to the top of the head, where the bald cap must be aligned.

Crystal Clear Acrylic Coating: Spray coating used to seal sculptures and for spraying on a fake beard when it is applied to a toughie head.

Cupid's Bow: The center area of the upper lip that appears to have two peaks and a valley.

Cut: A tear in the skin.

D

Damage: Harm or injury to an object or person.

Damp: Slightly wet.

Degrade: To lower in quality.

Depression: A hollow on a surface.

Depth: Deepness, a measurement from the top down.

Dismantle: To take apart.

Dissolve: To turn a solid into a liquid.

Drag: To pull along with effort.

Drop Shadow: Used to create the illusion of a thick lower lash line. Can be applied with eyeshadow, eye pencil, or liquid liner.

E

Entrance Wound: Injury caused by a bullet entering the body.

Epoxy Parafilm: A spray release agent used to de-mold gelatin appliances.

Exit Wound: Injury caused by a bullet leaving the body.

Eyebrow: A group of hairs that grow above the eye, on the brow bone or supercillary arch.

Eyebrow Pencil: A make-up pencil used to shape, define, and fill in the eyebrow.

Eye Fold: The space between the upper lid line and under the eyebrow. Folds can either be one of or any combination of the following: slight fold, flat eye, recessed eye, heavy fold, asian slight fold, or asian heavy fold.

Eyeliner: A make-up product that is used to shape, add definition, and enhance the eye. Liquid, pencil, and eyeshadow may be used as eyeliners.

Eyeshadow: A colored powder make-up used to enhance, highlight, and shade the eyes.

Eye Pencil: A make-up pencil used to shape, define, and enhance the eyes.

F

Face Chart: A chart used to design or maintain the look of a character.

Fatty Tissue: Area above the eye that begins to hang down as we age.

Feathered: To blend something carefully into the skin.

Filbert Brush: A rounded and tapered brush typically used to apply eye shadow.

Fixer Spray: A thin sealer used to seal wax constructions and the edge of a vinyl bald cap.

Flashing: The excess material that surrounds an unapplied prosthetic appliance.

Flexible Collodion: Plastic sealer used to seal wax constructions and the edge of a vinyl bald cap.

Flocking: Rayon fibers cut into small pieces and used to color gelatin and silicone.

Foam Latex: A material used for prosthetic appliances.

Fossa: A depression in the skull.

Foundation: A make-up product that evens out the skin, toning down slight imperfections and flaws. It also refers to the entire process of base, highlight, shadow, concealer, and powder application.

Frontal Bone: The forehead bone.

Fumed Silica: Silicon Dioxide that has been exuded.

G

Gaf-quat: Super strong hair gel.

Gaunt: Very lean or haggard.

Gelatin: Transparent jelly-like substance derived from skin, tendons, etc., used in cooking and photography.

Glycerin: A thick, sweet, and colorless liquid used in medicine, ointment, hair products, and cosmetics.

H

Hackle: A piece of wood or metal with a series of closely placed pins, set-up in rows that are used like a giant comb to de-tangle most types of hair.

Hair Punching Needle: A needle used to push hair into artificial skin.

Hair White: Product used to turn normal hair into gray hair.

Hard Edge: A sharp division between highlight and shadow.

Hash Marks: Haphazard lines quickly drawn on the face.

Headshot: An 8x10 professional photograph of an actor.

Highlight: A light colored or reflective area.

I

Ice Powder: A product used to re-create the effect of ice and s now on the face.

Indented scar: A scar that has created a depression in the skin.

Injury: Harm or damage to the skin.

Ink Blot Pencil: An artist pencil used to make tattoo transfers on newsprint paper.

Internal Bleeding: Bleeding inside the body.

Iridescent: Reflects light and has shine.

J

Jagged: Unevenly cut or torn.

Jowl: Fleshy part of the jaw line.

K

Keloid: A raised scar.

Knead: To press, fold, and squeeze something.

K-Y Jelly: A brand of personal lubricant used to remove excess powder.

L

Labial Roll: A natural highlight that surrounds the edge of the lips. It adds dimension to the lip.

Lace: A fine, loose-weave material used to tie individual hairs to make a hairpiece.

Laceration: A tear in the skin.

Latex: Liquid rubber.

Liberal: To use a lot of something.

Lifecast: The process of taking an impression of someone's face or body.

Lip Line: The defined edge that surrounds the upper and lower lip.

Lipstick: A make-up product used to color lips. Lipstick comes in a wide variety of colors, formulas, and finishes.

Lip Gloss: A make-up product for the lips that is thicker than lipstick, and imparts a high shine. Can be worn alone, over lip liner, or over lipstick.

Lip Liner: A make-up pencil used to shape, define, and color lips.

M

Mascara: Eye make-up product that colors, lengthens, and thickens the eyelashes. Available in a variety of colors and formulas.

M.E.K.: Methyl Ethel Ketone; A harsh solvent.

Mandible: Lower jaw of humans.

Matte: Has no shine.

Matte Medium: Clear acrylic material used to matte acrylic paint.

Maxilla: Upper jaw of humans.

Mold: A hollow container into which a substance, such as foam latex, is poured or injected.

Morgue: A collection of photographs for the purpose of reference.

Mortician's Wax: A pliable material used as a sculpting material on the face.

Mortuary: A room or building in which dead bodies are kept until burial.

Mustache: Facial hair above the upper lip.

Mush: To smash or squash.

Mustard Yellow: A muted yellow color used to add olive to a base color.

N

Nape of the Neck: The back of the neck.

Naphtha: Lighter fluid; used to help dissolve the edge of a rubber bald cap.

Nasolabial Fold: The crease that runs from above the nostril to just out from the corner of the mouth.

Negative Mold: The mold half that is the reverse shape of a prosthetic appliance.

Nostrils: Either of the two openings of the nose.

Nozzle: The tip of the airbrush.

O

Occipital: The protruding bone on the back of the head.

Olive: A yellow green colored undertone.

Opaque: Impossible to see through.

Orange Stipple Sponge: A large celled sponge used to stipple color into the skin.

Overlay Drawing: A design tracing to help production understand what a character may look like.

P

Paasche: An airbrush manufacturer.

Paint & Powder: Terminology used to describe the process of aging with color.

Palette: A metal, wax paper, or acrylic piece used as a holding area for make-up.

Palette Knife: Artist knife used to sculpt wax and to scoop make-up from containers.

Pax Paint: Pros-aide, acrylic paint, and Matte Medium mixed together to make a very sticky paint for prosthetics.

Photoshop: A computer program used to alter photographs for design reasons.

Pigment: Coloring matter usually in powder form and mixed with oils, water, etc. to create a colored make-up.

Pigmented Powder: Talc and pigment mixed together to form a translucent powder.

Plastic Beard: A beard made on a toughie head and sprayed with a plastic spray for the purpose of removing the beard and re-applying it to an actor.

Plastic Sealer: Sealer used to seal wax constructions and the edge of a vinyl bald cap.

Plastic Spray: Spray coating used to seal sculptures and for spraying on a fake beard when it is applied to a toughie head.

Pliable: Able to bend or move easily.

Pliatex Mold Rubber: Latex used for making bald caps and molds.

Powder: Talc that is used for setting make-up and decreasing shine.

Powder Puff: A velour pad used to hold powder.

Precautions: Care taken before hand to avoid risk or injury.

Primary Colors: Red, Blue, and Yellow.

Producer: The maker of the movie, and usually the person funding it.

Production: Term used to describe a film company.

Pros-aide: A white acrylic adhesive used to apply prosthetics. It dries clear.

Prosthetic Appliance: Foam latex, gelatin, or silicone piece used to change the features of an actor's face.

Pucker: To gather together.

Puddle: A small pool.

R

Random: Without method or conscious choice.

Rayon Flocking: Fibers cut into small pieces and used to color gelatin and silicone.

Release Agent: A separator for molds and prosthetics.

Rigid Collodion: A material used to create indented scars.

Roughing Out: Terminology used to describe the first steps of sculpting.

Rubber: A tough elastic substance made from latex of plants or synthetically.

Rubber Cement: A common type of glue used to mix with pigment in order to create a paint that will stick to urethane foams.

Rubber Mask Grease Paint: Castor oil based cream make-up designed for use on all rubber products.

Ruddy: A reddish undertone.

Runny: Very easy to flow.

S

Sanitation: The maintenance of sanitary conditions.

Scar: An old healed cut.

Scrape: An injury to the skin caused by friction.

Scratch: A small cut.

Sculpture: The art of making three-dimensional forms.

Severe: Very harsh.

Shade: The value of lightness/darkness of a color.

Shadow: To darken or cast by an object between a light source and a subject.

Shine: A highly reflective spot or area caused by moisture or perspiration.

Shrink: To make smaller.

Sideburn: Facial hair in front of the ears.

Silicone Adhesive: Telesis adhesive.

Silicone Caulk: Clear caulk used to seal windows and bathtubs. We use it as a paint system for silicone skins.

Silicone G.F.A.: Gel filled appliances, the most recent advance in prosthetics. Is used as an appliance.

Simulate: To re-create.

Skin Illustrator: A brand of alcohol based make-up.

Skin Tone: The color of skin. Usually a combination of shade and undertone mixed to match a person's skin color.

Slip: A term used in cosmetics to describe the consistency of a liquid or cream product. The more slip a product has, the creamier it feels.

Smashed: Squashed or mashed.

Smearing: To spread with force.

Soft Edge: The gradation between highlight and shadow.

Sorbitol: A preservative used in gelatin appliances that increase strength and stability.

Special Make-up Effects: Term used to describe make-up and effects that are not traditional forms of make-up application.

Spirit Gum: A resin based adhesive used mainly for hair work.

Stacolor: A brand of alcohol based make-up.

Stagey: An overly done make-up application.

Stipple: The process of applying make-up and the dotted pattern left by that process.

Subjective: An opinion; not impartial or literal.

Sunburn: Burn caused by overexposure to the sun.

Superficial: On the surface or not very deep.

Swelling: A raised injury to the skin.

Symmetry: Perfect balance between two sides.

Synthetic Hair: Artificially created hair usually made of plastic.

T

Tacky: Sticky.

Taper: To diminish as it moves away.

Tattoo: Permanent art on the skin.

Tattoo Ink: Alcohol based colors used to re-create tattoos.

Tear Duct: The duct in the innermost corner of the eye where tears are formed.

Telesis: A brand name of silicone adhesive.

Telesis Thinner: Product used to thin or lessen the strength of Telesis.

Temporal Fossa: Depression on each side of the forehead.

Thick: Firm in consistency

Three Dimensional: Height, Depth and Width.

Toughie Head: A face made of firm urethane used to practice beard application.

Translucent: Allowing light to pass through.

Transparent: Completely water clear.

Tuplast: A thick plastic material used to create blisters and scars.

Tweezers: A small tool used for grabbing small items.

Two Dimensional: Height and width, no depth.

U

Ultra Ice: Product designed to look like ice on the skin.

Undertone: The underlying color of the skin.

Urethane: Water-soluble crystalline compound.

V

Vehicle: The material that transports pigment. It is the element of make-up that gives it slip.

Veins: Any of the tubes conveying blood to the heart.

Ventilate: The process of hand-tying each hair to lace.

Ventilating Needle: The needle used in the process of hand tying each hair to lace.

Vinyl: Plastic material used to make bald caps.

Viscosity: Refers to the thickness of a liquid.

Volatile: Evaporates easily.

W

Wardrobe: Clothing worn by an actor in films.

Wax: A pliable material used as a sculpting material on the face.

White Sponge: A foam sponge used to apply make-up to a performer.

Witch Hazel: A mild astringent.

Woochie: A brand name of low cost latex appliances.

Wound: Injury to the skin.

Wrinkles: Lines and creases in the face caused by aging.

Y

Yak Hair: Hair from a large mammal called a Yak.

Z

Zinc Oxide: White pigment.

Zygomatic Arch: The Cheekbone.

Notes:

_____

_____

_____

_____

_____

_____

_____

_____

_____

PROFESSIONAL MAKE-UP SUPPLIERS

The following stores provide make-up materials to the professional make-up artist.
Some of these companies additionally provide student discounts.

Sally's Beauty Supply
11239 Ventura Blvd.
Studio City, CA 91604
Phone: (818) 508-0797

Cinema Secrets
4400 Riverside Drive
Burbank, CA 91505
Phone: (818) 846-0579

Naimies Beauty Supply
12640 Riverside Drive
N. Hollywood, CA 91606
Phone: (818) 655-9922

Frends Beauty Supply
5270 Laurel Canyon Blvd.
N. Hollywood, CA 91607
Phone: (818) 769-3834

Image Exclusives
8020 Melrose Avenue
W. Hollywood, CA 90046
Phone: (323) 651-5002

mudshop – LA
129 S. San Fernando Blvd.
Burbank, CA 91502
www.mudshop.com
Phone: (818) 729-9420

mudshop – NYC
375 West Broadway, Suite 202
New York, NY 10012
www.mudshop.com
Phone: (212) 925-9250

Burman Industries
14141 Covello St., #10-C
Van Nuys, CA 91405
Phone: (818) 782-9833
Fax: (818) 992-5337

Reel Creations, Inc.
7831 Alabama Ave., Unit 21
Canoga Park, CA 91304
Phone: (818) 348-2997
Fax: (818) 992-5337

Graftobian Theatrical
510 Tasman Street
Madison, WI 53714
1-800-255-0584
www.graftobian.com

Ben Nye Make-up, Inc.
5935 Bowcroft Street
Los Angeles, CA 90016
Phone: (310) 839-1984
Fax: (310) 839-2640

ADM TRONICS Unlimited, Inc.
224-S Pegasus Ave
Northvale, NJ 07647
Phone: 201 767 6040
Fax: 201 784 0620

Davis Dental
7347 Ethel Ave.
N. Hollywood, CA 91605
Phone: 818-765-4994
Fax: 818-765-5847

Factor II
P.O. Box 1339
Lakeside, AZ 85929
Phone: 800-332-8688
Fax: 520-537-8066

Fibreglast
1944 Neva Dr.
Dayton, Oh 45414
Phone: 800-821-3283
Fax: 937-833-6555

Laguna Clay Co.
14400 Lomitas Ave.
Industry, CA
Phone: 626-330-0631
Fax: 626-333-7694

PolyTech
949 Fairway
City of Industry, CA 91789
Phone: 909 594 2300

Sculpture House
Phone: 609-466-2986
Fax: 609-466-2450

Silpak
10611 Burbank Blvd.
Burbank, CA
Phone: 818 985 8850
Fax: 818 985 5658

Tower Hobbies
P.O. Box 9078City, State:
Champaign, IL
Phone: 800-637-4989
Fax: 800-637-7303

Tri-ess Sciences
1020 W. Chestnut St.
Burbank, CA 91506
Phone: 800-274-6910
Fax: 818-848-3521

Van Dykes
P.O. Box 278
Woonsocket, SD 57385
Phone: 800-843-3320
Fax: 605-796-4085

Other:

_____

_____

_____

_____

_____

_____

_____

_____

_____

_____

Make-up Designory's Beauty Make-up
by Yvonne Hawker and John Bailey,
Make-up Designory, Burbank, CA 2004   ISBN 0-9749500-1-7

Stage Makeup: Eighth Edition, by Richard Corson. Prentice-Hall, Englewood Cliffs, New Jersey, 1986   ISBN 0-13-840521-2

Fashions In Makeup, by Richard Corson. Peter Owen
Limited, London   ISBN 0-7206-0431-1

Fashions In Hair, by Richard Corson. Peter Owen Limited,
London   ISBN 0-7206-3283-8

Fashions In Eyeglasses, by Richard Corson.
Peter Owen Limited, London

The Technique of the Professional Make-up for Film, Television and Stage, by Vincent J-R Kehoe.
Focal Press, Boston 1985   ISBN 0-240-51244-8

Special Makeup Effects, by Vincent J-R Kehoe. Focal Press,
Boston, 1991   ISBN 0-240-80099-0

Techniques of Three Dimensional Make-up, by Lee
Baygan. Watson-Guptill Publications,
New York 1988   ISBN 0-8230-5261-3

The Complete Make-up Artist, by Penny Delamar.
Northwestern University Press,
Evanston 1997   ISBN 0-8101-1258-2

Making Faces:
A Complete Guide to Face Painting, by Sian Ellis-Thomas
Sunburst Books, London   ISBN 1-85778-238-0

The Art of Make-up, by Kevyn Aucoin. Harper Collins
Publishers, Callaway Editions 1994   ISBN 0-06-017186-3

Making Faces, by Kevyn Aucoin. Little, Brown & Company,
Boston 1997   ISBN 0-316-28686-9

***Fine Beauty: Beauty Basics and Beyond
for African-American Women***, by Sam Fine. Riverhead
Books, New York 1998   ISBN 1-57322-095-7

Hollywood Glamour Portraits, by John Kobal (editor).
Dover Publications, New York, 1976   ISBN 0-486-23352-9

***Behind The Mask: The Secrets of Hollywood's
Monster Masks***, by Mark Salisbury and Alan Hedgecock.
Titan Books, London, 1994   ISBN 1-85286-488-5

***Men, Makeup and Monsters: Hollywood's Masters
of Illusion and FX***, by Anthony Timpone. St. Martin's Press,
New York, 1996   ISBN 0-312-14678-7

Do It Yourself - Monster Makeup Handbook, by Dick
Smith. Imagine, Inc., Pittsburgh, 1985   ISBN 0-911137-02-5

How To Draw Animals, by Jack Hamm. Perigee Books
Putnam Publishing Group. NY, NY   ISBN 0-399-50802-3

After Ninety, by Imogen Cunningham.
(paperback)   ISBN 0-295-95673-9

Barlowe's Guide to Fantasy, by Wayne Douglas Barlowe.
(paperback)   ISBN 0-06-100817-6

The Source book: Props, Set Dressing & Wardrobe,
Debbie's Book, 2000   ISBN 0-9637404-6-6

The Artist's Way, by Julie Cameron

Drawing on the Right Side of the Brain,
by Betty Edwards. Jeremy P. Tarcher, Inc. ISBN 0-87477-523-X

The Mane Thing, by Kevin Mancuso. ISBN 0-316-166-146

Drawing the Human Head, by Burne Hogarth. Watson-Guptill Publications   ISBN 0-8230-1375-8

An Atlas of Anatomy for Artists,
by Fritz Schider. Dover Publication,Inc.   ISBN 486-20241-0

Gray's Anatomy, by Henry Gray, F.R.S., ISBN 0-914294-49-0

1940's Hairstyles, by Daniela Turudich.
Streamline Press   ISBN 930064-01-2

Vintage Weddings, Streamline Press

Face Forward, by Kevin Aucion

Design Your Face, by Way Bandy

The Face of a Century, by Kate De Castelbajac

Film and Television Makeup, by Herman Buchman.
Watson-Guptill Publications   ISBN 0-8230-7560-50

The Face is a Canvas, by Irene Corey.
Anchorage Press, Inc.   ISBN 087602-031-7

Faces Fantasy Makeup, by Martin Jans and
Servaas Van Eijk.   ISBN 90-70659-03-4

Assoline, by Serge Lutens.   ISBN 2-84323-066-7

Il Trucco E La Mashero, by Stefano Anselmo
ISBN 88-85278-10-8

Art & Fear, by David Bayles & Ted Orland.
Capra Press   ISBN 0-88496-379-9

Magazines

Make-up Artist Magazine

Cinefantastique

Rue Morgue

Daily Variety

Hollywood Reporter

Mercury Production Report

Allure

Marie Claire

Instyle

Inspire Quarterly

Modern Salon

American Salon

Elle

Cosmopolitan

Other:

_____   _____

_____   _____

_____   _____

_____   _____

_____   _____

_____   _____

_____   _____

WORD INDEX

Make-up Designory has evolved in both business size and reputation. From its original two-room school in 1998, Make-up Designory has grown to become one of the largest and most respected schools of its kind in the United States. Both Make-Up Designory campuses provide an educational center which contain modern classrooms, labs, video and photography areas, a student library, and a cosmetics boutique. In the Spring of 2003, Make-up Designory completed the strenuous requirements of national accreditation, being accredited and honored as a "Distinguished School" by the Accrediting Commission of Career Schools and Colleges of Technology (ACCSCT).

Make-up Designory's reputation attracts over 800 students a year from all parts of the world to its Los Angeles campus. Students enjoy courses in beauty, character, special make-up effects, set hairstyling, wardrobe styling and costume supervision. Make-up Designory's instructors have many years of professional experience and are certified by the State in which they teach. These instructors teach from a unique curriculum and pass on to their students practical and real world skills. Upon completion of their studies, Make-up Designory graduates go on to work and enjoy fruitful careers in the fashion, film, television, and cosmetics industries. In the Spring of 2005, Make-up Designory opened a second location in New York City. Situated in the trendy SoHo district, the facility offers a wide range of courses, as well as, a beautiful retail store providing Make-up Designory's unique line of products to both consumers and industry professionals.

Classes are offered year-round, with day and evening schedules available.
———————————————— Offered subjects are: ————————————————

- *Beauty Make-up Artistry Course*
- *Character Make-up Artistry Course*
- *Special Make-up Effects Course*
- *Studio Hairstyling Course*

- *Costume & Wardrobe Program*
- *Fashion Styling Program*
- *Journeyman Make-up Artistry Program*
- *Master Make-up Artistry Program*

If you would like more information, or to request a school catalog:
Call: 818-729-9420 for Burbank, CA or 212-925-9250 for New York, NY

Write:
Make-Up Designory
129 S. San Fernando Blvd.
Burbank, CA 91502
or
Make-Up Designory
375 W. Broadway, Ste. 202
New York, NY 10012

Surf the net:
www.makeupschool.com
www.makeupdesignory.com
www.mud.edu

**For information regarding
Make-up Designory products:**
call the mudshop at 818-557-7619
or 212-925-9250

shop online at:
www.mudshop.com